Maths Bank

ALAN BRIGHOUSE / DAVID GODBER / PETER PATILLA

LEVEL THREE

A teacher's resource for pupil assessment

Nelson

The authors and publishers are grateful for the help of:

Pauline Roberts
Eynsham Primary School
Eynsham Oxford

The extracts from *Mathematics in the National Curriculum* are reproduced with the permission of the Controller of Her Majesty's Stationery Office.

Thomas Nelson and Sons Ltd
Nelson House Mayfield Road
Walton-on-Thames Surrey
KT12 5PL UK

Thomas Nelson (Hong Kong) Ltd
Toppan Building 10/F
22A Westlands Road,
Quarry Bay Hong Kong

Thomas Nelson Australia
102 Dodds Street
South Melbourne
Victoria 3205
Australia

Nelson Canada
1120 Birchmount Road
Scarborough Ontario
M1K 5GF Canada

© A. Brighouse, D. Godber, P. Patilla 1992
First published by Thomas Nelson and Sons Ltd 1992

ISBN 0-17-421262-3
NPN 9 8 7 6 5 4 3 2

All rights reserved. This publication is protected in the United Kingdom by the Copyright, Design and Patents Act 1988 and in other countries by comparable legislation.

The publisher grants permission for copies of pages 9–44, 47–60, 63–78, 81–92, 95–208 to be made without fee as follows:
Private purchasers may make copies for their own use or for use by their own students; school purchasers may make copies for use within and by the staff and students of the school only. This permission to copy does not extent to additional schools or branches of an institution, who should purchase a separate master copy of the book for their own use.

For copying in any other circumstances prior permission in writing must be obtained from Thomas Nelson and Sons Ltd.

Printed in Great Britain

Contents

General Introduction   *4 – 6*

Number and Algebra
Introduction   *7*
Activities 1 – 54   *9 – 44*

Measures
Introduction   *45*
Activities 55 – 76   *47 – 60*

Shape and space
Introduction   *61*
Activities 77 – 102   *63 – 78*

Handling data
Introduction   *79*
Activities 103 – 127   *81 – 92*

Using and applying mathematics
Introduction   *93*
Activities 128 – 147   *95 – 108*

Appendix A   Pupil Mastersheets A1 – 75   *109 – 183*
Appendix B   Resource Mastersheets B1 – 8   *185 – 192*
Appendix C   Recording Mastersheets C1– 8   *193 – 200*
                  Record charts   *201 – 206*

Overview   *207 – 208*

The activities, appendices and overview may be photocopied.

General Introduction

The material

The material within this resource relates both to the programme of study and to the attainment targets for Level 3 of the Mathematics National Curriculum. It is provided to enable you to evaluate and record pupil progress. The resource offers you maximum flexibility:

- the activities can be done in any order
- there are a variety of activities for you to select from
- children can work independently
- co-operative small group work is possible
- children can work within a large group for some of the activities

This file is arranged differently from Levels 1 and 2. The 'notes for teachers' are now assembled at the front in five sections, while the 'evaluation sheets' (or Mastersheets) are at the back. The format of the 'notes' is as follows:

- **Aim:** indicating the focus of mathematics to which each activity relates
- **Notes:** giving helpful notes on connected activities in the appendices, and their rationale
- **Evaluation checkpoints:** giving suggested points to help you make detailed evaluation comments on each pupil
- **Activity:** detailing the setting up of each activity and what to look for when pupils are involved with it

The three sections at the back of the book describe resources for the activities as follows:

- **Pupil Mastersheets** (Appendix A) These are provided to support certain activities and are for pupils to work on and record their findings.
- **Resource Mastersheets** (Appendix B) These provide support materials in certain activities if suitable material is not available in the classroom.
- **Recording Mastersheets** (Appendix C) The first eight of these are for pupils and/or teachers to record what has been achieved in any given activity, and the last six are teacher record sheets.

National Curriculum

Much of the terminology of the National Curriculum consists of complex statements, for example:

'read, write and order numbers to at least 1000; use the knowledge that the position of a digit indicates its value'.

Some of the evaluations in the file will focus on just one of the components of such statements. The comments written under Aim (in Chapters 1–5) will show the focus. It may be necessary for several evaluations to be completed, each with a different focus, before you can be assured the child has fully achieved a particular statement.

The National Curriculum is a framework and as such omits to state some quite important 'mathematical targets'. Some of these 'missing targets' will contribute towards a child's subsequent understanding and are worthy of evaluation. For example, reference is made to the general names for 3, 5- and 6-sided shapes (triangles, pentagons, hexagons) but not to quadrilaterals, the general name for 4-sided shapes. There is reference to estimating and approximating quantity but there is no reference to estimating positions on number lines.

Some of the *Maths Bank* evaluations will include 'missing targets'.

The relationship between the *Maths Bank* activities and the National Curriculum Mathematics attainment targets is shown in the overview on pages 207 – 8.

Completed evaluation sheets can be used to support your assessment of a child's progress within the National Curriculum and can be used as firm evidence of pupil achievement as part of your Teacher Assessment.

The record charts comprise photocopiable record sheets to enable you to keep a record of which activities have been used with each child, and which attainment targets have been evaluated.

Using the Material

- In any one activity each pupil will need a sheet from Appendix A, B or C. Appendix A or C will form a permanent record of the activity.
- At the top of each of these sheets is an empty 'star' for you to write the number of the activity.
- It is assumed that the evaluations will be integrated into normal classroom activities and not be perceived as 'different' by children and teachers.
- How often you use the evaluations is a matter for your discretion.
- Given the complexity of some of the statements within the National Curriculum it would be inappropriate to attempt to determine pupil achievement on the basis of a single classroom activity. As a consequence many of the evaluations in the file offer the opportunity to focus on particular elements of more complex statements. The evaluations are essentially intended to support ongoing assessment rather than provide summative 'end of key stage' assessments.
- The evaluation sheets are intended to be used in any order and whenever it is judged appropriate. The charts in Appendix C will help you keep a record of which activities have been used with each child.
- Although most of the activities focus on one particular aspect of the Mathematics National Curriculum often other elements, particularly Using and applying mathematics, will be evident and can be commented upon.
- Many of the activities also offer potential for cross-curricular evaluation (for example, English attainment targets). Include relevant comments on other areas of the curriculum whenever you feel it is appropriate to do so.
- There is space provided on the bottom of each Mastersheet A or C for your evaluation comments. Also at the bottom of sheets A1 – 67 is a summary of the focus of the evaluation, but it is expected that you will record further details based on the advice and comments provided in the relevant notes for each activity (Chapters 1 – 5). When completed each evaluation sheet becomes a valuable part of a pupil's profile of work, providing hard evidence of progress, no matter how small.
- For some of the activities simple pieces of apparatus should be used as part of the evaluation. Some of this simple apparatus, such as digit cards, is provided in the form of Resource Mastersheets (Appendix B) in case they are not available in the classroom. Other activities will require commonly-used

classroom apparatus for the evaluation (for example, Multilink cubes). In these activities, pupils record their results on one of the Recording Mastersheets in Appendix C: C1 has a squared recording area, C2 has a lined recording area and C3 has a blank recording area. There is space allocated on all these Recording Mastersheets for your evaluation comments. Because of the multipurpose nature of the Appendix C sheets, the summary of the focus of each evaluation has been omitted: please refer instead to the activity in the 'notes for teachers' section.

- Mastersheet C4 is a general purpose teacher observation sheet for you to comment on the small number of activities that use neither Appendix A nor C1 – 3 Mastersheets.
- Mastersheets C5 – 8 relate specifically to given activities and have space allocated for your evaluation comments.
- Children should have free access to apparatus for any activity. Recording both the use and misuse of apparatus is a valid part of the evaluation.
- It is not expected that all the activities will be done by each child or group of children. The range of activities is there for the teacher to choose from. This wide choice also allows for further evaluation of the same aspect of the curriculum using a different activity.
- It is assumed that activities will not be attempted by children without some teacher presence during at least part of the time, to introduce, observe and discuss.

Evaluation and recording

- It is generally possible to evaluate several individuals within a group activity. It may be appropriate therefore for several children to do the same activity from this file at the same time, in order to facilitate your evaluation of them.
- Many of the activities offer an opportunity for you to observe how children undertake certain tasks as part of the overall evaluation.
- For some activities children may record their results with apparatus and may well need prompting to produce a permanent record by drawing and/or using symbols where this is to form part of the evaluation.
- Relevant observations and anecdotal records need to be made about each activity completed by each child. These can be recorded on:

    the space provided on each Pupil Mastersheet (A1 – 75),

    or the space provided on the Pupil Recording Mastersheet (C1 – 3),

    or the teacher observation sheet (C4).

    Photographs of an activity could also be added to the pupil's portfolio.
- Although all the evaluation sheets in this resource are labelled Level 3, many children will approach the suggested activities using skills, language and knowledge appropriate to higher levels. This is to be expected and should be noted in your comments.

Summary

You might find it helpful to think of the following steps when using this file:

1 Choose an activity from chapters 1 – 5 and refer to Appendix A, B and/or C.
2 Assemble the materials.
3 Conduct the activity, referring to the 'notes for teachers' and evaluation checkpoints.
4 Record evaluation comments in the space provided.

Number and Algebra

Introduction

The Number and Algebra activities assess whether pupils are able to:

- read, write and order numbers to at least 1000; use the knowledge that the position of a digit indicates its value.
- use decimal notation as the conventional way of recording in money
- appreciate the meaning of negative whole numbers in familiar contexts
- know and use addition and subtraction number facts to 20 (including zero)
- solve problems involving multiplication or division of whole numbers or money, using a calculator where necessary
- know and use multiplication facts up to 5 x 5, and all those in 2, 5 and 10 multiplication tables
- recognise that the first digit is the most important in indicating the size of a number, and approximate to the nearest 10 or 100
- understand 'remainders' given the context of calculation, and know whether to round up or down
- explain number patterns and predict subsequent number where appropriate
- find number patterns and equivalent forms of 2-digit numbers and use these to perform mental calculations
- recognise whole numbers which are exactly divisible by 2, 5 and 10
- deal with inputs to and outputs from simple function machines

The grouping of the activities is shown overleaf, while their relationship to the National Curriculum statements of attainment is shown on pp. 207 – 8.

- There are two aspects of number evaluated in the activities in this chapter:
  - **i** cardinal aspect, which is concerned with the value of a number
  - **ii** positional aspect, which is concerned with the position of a number on a number line.

Both these aspects are important in developing pupil understanding of number.

- When pupils are adding and subtracting small numbers it is worth considering how they obtain the results:
  - **i** by counting all
  - **ii** by counting on from the first number
  - **iii** by counting on from the larger number
  - **iv** by taking away
  - **v** by counting back
  - **vi** by counting on
  - **vii** by quick recall

- For pupils to be able to add and subtract small numbers at Level 3 they ought to recognise relationships rather than just remember the number facts as separate entities. They should, for instance:
  - **i** recognise that addition is commutative, for example, 2 + 6 = 6 + 2 = 8
  - **ii** know addition/subtraction trios rather than separate number facts, such

as the 3, 4, 7 +/– trio: 3 + 4 = 7, 4 + 3 = 7, 7 – 3 = 4, 7 – 4 = 3

   iii be able to transfer a number bond onto an extended number line such as:
3 + 4 = 7, 13 + 4 = 17, 23 + 4 = 27, 33 + 4 = 37

   iv appreciate that addition and subtraction are inverses, for example:
if 12 – 7 = 5 then 5 + 7 = 12

   v recognise the relationship between odd and even numbers, such as:
O + O = E

- Pupils' understanding of both the repeated addition and array aspects of multiplication is evaluated, for example:

3 x 4 = 3 + 3+ 3 + 3 (repeated addition)

3 x 4 =  (array pattern)

Understanding the commutative property of multiplication is also evaluated.

- Pupils' appreciation that division also has different aspects (such as repeated subtraction and equal sharing) is evaluated, for example:

18 ÷ 3 = 18 – 3 – 3 – 3 – 3 – 3 – 3; six threes in 18 (repeated subtraction)

18 ÷ 3 = 3 sets of 6 (equal sharing)

Pages 9 – 44 may be photocopied

Activities 1 – 54

The Number and Algebra activities are grouped as follows:

Activities Statements

    1 – 12 read, write and order numbers to at least 1000; use the knowledge that the position of a digit indicates its value.

  13 – 15 use decimal notation as the conventional way of recording in money

  16 – 18 appreciate the meaning of negative whole numbers in familiar contexts

  19 – 27 know and use addition and subtraction number facts to 20 (including zero)

  28 – 30 solve problems involving multiplication or division of whole numbers or money, using a calculator where necessary

  31 – 33 know and use multiplication facts up to 5x5, and all those in 2, 5 and 10 multiplication tables

  34 – 38 recognise that the first digit is the most important in indicating the size of a number, and approximate to the nearest 10 or 100

  39 – 41 understand 'remainders' given the context of calculation, and know whether to round up or down

  42 – 45 explain number patterns and predict subsequent number where appropriate.

  46 – 48 find number patterns and equivalent forms of 2-digit numbers and use these to perform mental calculations

  49 – 51 recognise whole numbers which are exactly divisible by 2, 5 and 10

  52 – 54 deal with inputs to and outputs from simple function machines

Notes for Teachers

Activities 1 – 2

Aim
▲ to read, write and order numbers to at least 1000
▲ to use the knowledge that the position of a digit indicates its value

Notes
▲ Activities 1 and 2 require pupils to make 3-digit numbers using a 'fan' of digits. The criteria for making each number involves both the cardinal aspect of number (for example, largest numbers and smallest numbers) and the positional aspect of number (for example, numbers nearest to 500).

▲ Pupils cut out the individual 'fan digits' and make a fan with them using a brass paper fastener.

▲ When making numbers with the fan digits, the top digit (for example, digit 4 in Activity 1) need not necessarily be the first digit in a number.

▲ Pupils should also realise that they are not allowed to have any digit in the fan 'dangling down' so that the top digit on each fan will always form part of the number being made.

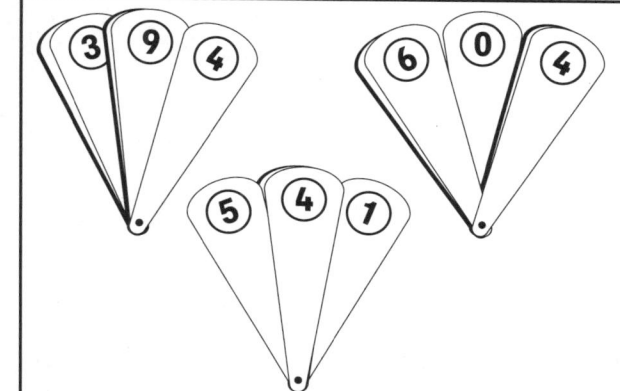

Evaluation checkpoints
▲ can read 3-digit numbers
▲ can write 3-digit numbers
▲ can order 3-digit numbers
▲ understands that the position of a digit indicates its value
▲ understands cardinal language of number
▲ understands positional language of number

Materials: *Mastersheet B1 (p.185) copied onto thin card*

● Pupils should put the digit 4 as the top number on the fan, the other digits in any order.

● Ask them to show you various 3-digit numbers with their fans according to certain cardinal number criteria such as:

the largest 3-digit number (984);

or the positional aspect of number such as:

the number nearest to 500 (498);

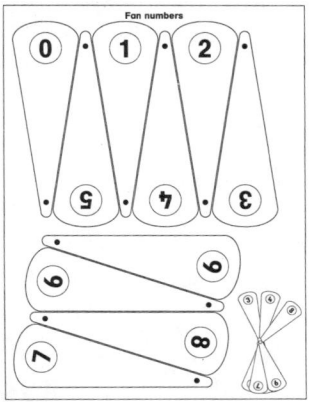

B1

Maths Bank : Level 3   Number   Page 9

NOTES FOR TEACHERS

Activities 1 – 2 continued

Pupils will notice throughout this activity that the digit 4 will always have to be part of the number shown.

- Pupils can record their results with pencil and paper on C1, C2 or C3.
- The top digit on the fan can be changed for a different one, for example 6.

2 *Materials:* As for Activity 1

- Each member of a group could have a different top digit on his/her fan and the group could then compare and order their results when asked to make numbers according to different criteria such as in Activity 1.

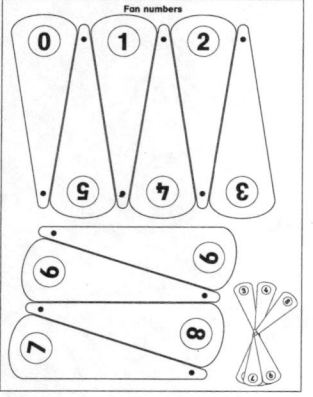

B1

Notes for Teachers

Activities 3 – 5

Aim
▲ to read, write and order numbers to at least 1000
▲ to use the knowledge that the position of a digit indicates its value

Notes
▲ The following three activities require pupils to make 3-digit numbers using a set of individual digit cards. As in Activities 1 and 2, the criteria for making each number involves both the cardinal aspect and the positional aspect of number.
▲ It is possible to use these evaluation activities with a group of pupils.
▲ Pupils cut out the individual digits.

Evaluation checkpoints
▲ can read 3-digit numbers
▲ can order 3-digit numbers
▲ understands that the position of a digit indicates its value
▲ understands that a three-digit number lies between 99 and 1000
▲ can write 3-digit numbers

3 *Materials: Mastersheet B2 (p.186) copied onto thin card*

- Pupils choose any set of four digits from the set of cards cut out from Mastersheet B2, for example:

They then make as many different 3-digit numbers as they can, such as:
245, 485, 524, 824

- The results can be shown on one of the Recording Mastersheets (C1, C2 or C3, pp. 193 – 5) and the set of numbers ordered from the smallest to largest number.

- Question what would happen if one of the digits selected was zero. This should lead to a discussion as to whether the digit 0 should be discounted where it is a first digit. Pupils should appreciate that 3-digit numbers lie between 99 and 1000.

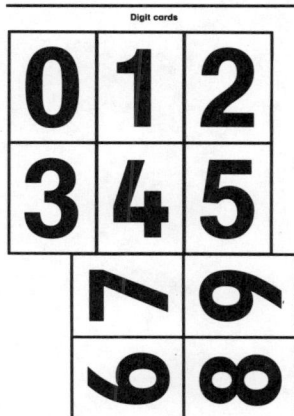

B2

MATHS BANK: Level 3   Number   Page 11

NOTES FOR TEACHERS

Activities 3 – 5 continued

Materials: *As for Activity 3*

- Oral activities can be carried out with a group or class of pupils using the digit cards, for example: *'Show me two hundred and forty three.' 'Make it 10 more; 20 less.'*

Care needs to be taken not to include numbers which require two or more identical digits to be used, for example 242.

Materials: *As for Activity 3*

- Members of a group each make a different 3-digit number. Each pupil needs to be able to see all the numbers made. Without allowing group discussion, or any form of help, ask questions such as: *'Who has the largest number?' 'Which number(s) is odd/even?'*

The pupil who considers his/her number is the answer responds by holding up a hand.

NOTES FOR TEACHERS

Activities 6 – 8

Aim
▲ to read, write and order numbers to at least 1000
▲ to use the knowledge that the position of a digit indicates its value

Notes
▲ If 3-spike abaci are not available then counters can be placed on Mastersheet A1 instead.
▲ The activities may be used with a group of pupils and individual evaluations made.
▲ Pupils use Mastersheet C1, C2 or C3 (pp.193 – 5) to record results.

Evaluation checkpoints
▲ able to read, write and order 3-digit numbers
▲ understands that the position of a digit indicates its value

6 *Materials: a 3-spike abacus or Mastersheet A1 (p.109)*
- 'Show me' activities can be undertaken where pupils place beads or counters on their abaci to represent any number you state. Pupils should be able to record numbers made and orally to state each number they record.

7 *Materials: a 3-spike abacus or Mastersheet A1*
- Restrict to three the number of beads or counters which can be placed on each abacus. Students then have to make different numbers using three beads or counters; the possibilities being: 3, 12, 21, 30, 102, 111, 120, 201, 210, 300.

  These numbers can then be ordered and sorted, for example into odds and evens (Number/Algebra).
  Similarly four and five beads or counters can be used on the abaci.

8 *Materials: a 3-spike abacus or Mastersheet A1*
- Pupils show a nominated number on their abaci and then alter this number according to given criteria, such as: make it 10 more; make it 3 less.
- By observing the techniques used by pupils it should become evident whether there is an appreciation of the fact that the position of a digit affects its value.

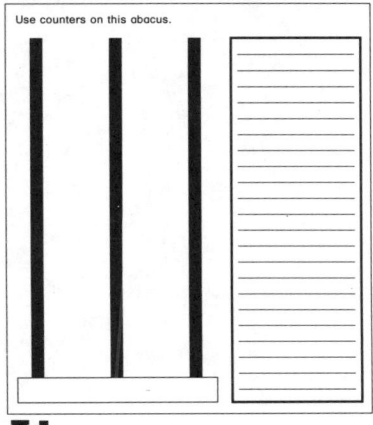

A1

MATHS BANK: Level 3 Number Page 13

Notes for Teachers

Activities 9 – 10

Aim
▲ to read, write and order numbers to at least 1000
▲ to use the knowledge that the position of a digit indicates its value

Notes
▲ Activities 9 and 10 use number lines to evaluate pupil understanding of place value: two types of number line are used, one on Mastersheet A2 and another on Mastersheet A3. A2 shows lines which have only ten divisions on them whereas A3 shows number lines with ten main divisions, each main division being further subdivided into ten parts.

▲ The number lines have no numbers on them thus allowing you to choose your own start and finish numbers. It is worthwhile starting some number lines at numbers other than zero.

▲ Given a starting number and a finishing number, pupils should initially work out the value of each division before trying to place nominated numbers on each line.

Evaluation checkpoints
▲ can read 3-digit numbers
▲ can write 3-digit numbers
▲ can order 3-digit numbers
▲ understands that the position of a digit indicates its value
▲ able to find positions on a number line
▲ able to calculate value of divisions on a number line

9 Materials: *Mastersheet A2 (p.110)*

● Pupils begin by writing a number of your choice (say 140) at the start of a line and another (say 150) at the end of the line. They then have to show where on the line other nominated numbers are, such as 146.

● By changing the start and finish numbers each subdivision can be given a different value, for example:

start number: 140	finish number: 150	each division: 1
start number: 100	finish number: 120	each division: 2
start number: 150	finish number: 200	each division: 5
start number: 0	finish number: 100	each division: 10
start number: 0	finish number: 1000	each division: 100

A2

Page 14 — Number — MATHS BANK: Level 3

NOTES FOR TEACHERS — Activities 9 – 10 continued

Ask children to indicate the position of numbers which are either on or between the subdivision marks.

 Materials: *Mastersheet A3 (p.111)*

- Activity 9 can be repeated using Mastersheet A3 which has each main subdivision on the number lines divided into 10 further divisions.

A3

NOTES FOR TEACHERS

Activities 11 – 12

Aim
▲ to read, write and order numbers to at least 1000
▲ to use the knowledge that the position of a digit indicates its value

Notes
▲ Activities 11 and 12 use MAB base 10 materials to allow pupils to represent numbers so as to show their 'value'. If MAB Base 10 materials are not available Mastersheet B3 can be photocopied onto thin card and the pieces cut out to represent hundreds, tens and units.
▲ When the pupils are making the numbers check that they are able to put the numbers into words.
▲ Observations and evaluations can be made on the teacher evaluation Mastersheet C4.

Evaluation checkpoints
▲ can read 3-digit numbers
▲ can write 3-digit numbers
▲ can orally state 3-digit numbers
▲ understands that the position of a digit indicates its value
▲ able to represent 3-digit numbers with apparatus
▲ able to represent 3-digit numbers by drawing

11 **Materials:** *MAB Base 10 material (or Mastersheet B3, p.187)*

• 'Show me' activities can be done with groups of pupils using the MAB apparatus to represent randomly chosen numbers, for example: *'Show me four hundred and three'*.

• An equivalence sheet divided into hundreds, tens and units columns can be used if you wish.

hundreds	tens	units

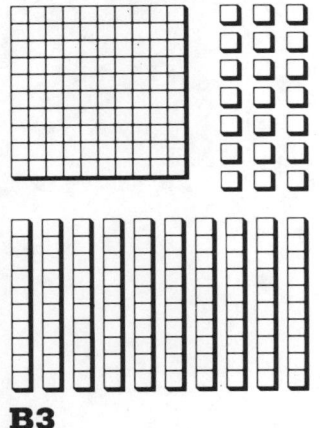

B3

Page 16   Number   MATHS BANK: Level 3

NOTES FOR TEACHERS

Activities 11 – 12 continued

Materials: *Mastersheet A5 (p.113)*

- Pupils are asked to record with numerals the numbers represented by MAB apparatus. They are then asked to 'draw' numbers, the drawings being representations of the MAB apparatus. Accept freehand sketches without the individual units being shown on the hundreds and tens.

- Ask the children to say some of the numbers so that you can check whether or not they are able to put numbers into words.

NOTES FOR TEACHERS

Activities 13 – 15

Aim
▲ to use decimal notation as the conventional way of recording in money

Notes
▲ The following three activities evaluate whether pupils can use decimal notation to record totals of money. Three aspects are considered:
  – recording amounts of money using decimal notation
  – mapping prices to coin equivalents
  – interpreting calculator displays as amounts of money.

▲ Real or plastic money may be used in these activities. Whether or not children choose to use money should form part of the evaluation.

Evaluation checkpoints
▲ able to record money using decimal notation
▲ able to interpret calculator display as decimal notation

Materials: *Mastersheet A6 (p.114)*
● Pupils record how much there is in each purse using decimal notation.

Materials: *Mastersheet A7 (p.115)*
● Pupils map the pictures of 'objects' to their equivalent costs in the purses.

Materials: *Mastersheet A8 (p.116)*
● Mastersheet A8 shows calculator displays of money totals for children to interpret. This activity is particularly good at evaluating children's understanding of the link between the decimal point which separates pounds and pennies (for example, £1.50) and the decimal point which acts as a true decimal (for example, £1.5).

A6 **A7** **A8**

Page 18   Number   MATHS BANK: Level 3

NOTES FOR TEACHERS

Activities 16 – 18

Aim
▲ to appreciate the meaning of negative whole numbers in familiar contexts

Notes
▲ The following three activities consider the use of negative numbers in three contexts:
- as thermometer readings
- as positions on a number line
- as negative readings on a calculator.

Evaluation checkpoints
▲ can read negative temperatures on thermometers
▲ can read negative positions on number lines
▲ can read simple scales on number lines, involving negative numbers
▲ understands negative output on a calculator
▲ understands negative results obtained by counting back

Materials: *Mastersheet A9 (p.117)*

● Mastersheet A9 shows several thermometers for children to interpret and record the temperatures. Once this has been undertaken you can ask them questions such as:

'Which shows the coldest temperature?'

'Which show temperatures warmer than this one?'

Materials: *Mastersheet A10 (p.118)*

● Mastersheet A10 shows several number lines with negative numbers as part of the range of numbers. Note that the segments on each line do not necessarily each represent 1. Pupils will have to work out the scale of each line before interpreting the position of the relevant arrow.

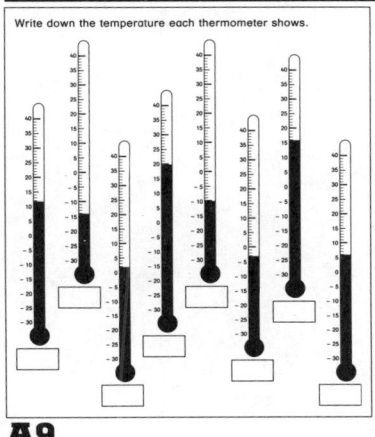

A9

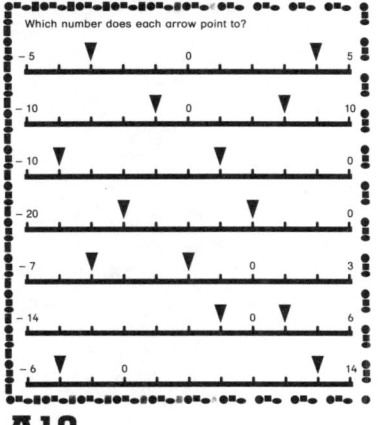

A10

MATHS BANK: Level 3 Number Page 19

NOTES FOR TEACHERS

Activities 16 – 18 continued

18 **Materials:** *Mastersheet A11 (p.119)*

- You could help a pupil towards understanding negative output on a calculator by linking this to counting back on a number line, for instance:

start at 4, count back 7, you land on – 3.

On a calculator: 4 – 7 = – 3

- On Mastersheet A11 pupils should interpret the calculator touches on the number lines.

A11

Page 20   Number   MATHS BANK : Level 3

NOTES FOR TEACHERS

Activities 19 – 22

Aim
▲ to know and use addition and subtraction number facts to 20

Notes
▲ The following four activities will involve pupils in totalling pairs of numbers, in finding the difference between numbers and in totalling more than two numbers.

▲ Each pupil will need several copies of Mastersheet A12 for the activities.

Evaluation checkpoints
▲ knows addition bonds to 20
▲ knows subtraction bonds to 20
▲ knows number bonds by quick recall
▲ can total more than two numbers

19 **Materials:** *Mastersheet A12 (p.120)*
- Choose a random total less than 18.
- Pupils find adjacent pairs of digits which have this total and then colour them. The 'digit pairs' can be horizontal or vertical: diagonal 'digit pairs' can be permitted if you wish.
- Observe whether totalling is by 'quick recall' of number facts or by some counting strategy.
- The given total can be varied.

20 **Materials:** *Mastersheet A12*
- Choose a random 'difference' which is less than 9.
- Pupils find 'digit pairs' which have this difference.
- Observe whether the calculation is by 'quick recall' of number facts or by some counting strategy.
- The given 'difference' can be varied.

Digit grid

6	4	2	1	0	3	7	8
9	5	3	5	6	1	2	9
4	8	7	3	0	9	2	4
5	5	8	7	1	4	6	2
6	7	6	1	8	4	5	3
9	9	3	5	8	0	2	1
7	4	3	8	0	4	2	9
8	5	3	3	7	6	2	1
5	9	7	4	5	5	0	8
6	6	8	4	5	9	9	2

A12

MATHS BANK: Level 3   Number

NOTES FOR TEACHERS

Activities 19 – 22 continued

Materials: *Mastersheet A12*

- Choose a random number which is less than 9.
- Pupils find 'digit pairs' which either have this total or this difference. Addition pairs could be coloured in one colour and difference pairs in another colour.

Materials: *Mastersheet A12*

- Choose a random total up to 20.
- Pupils find chains of digits which have this total. A 'digit chain' has more than two 'links' (i.e. digits); it can include both vertical and horizontal links but not diagonal links.
- This activity involves the students in adding more than two numbers to reach a total.

Digit grid

6	4	2	1	0	3	7	8
9	5	3	5	6	1	2	9
4	8	7	3	0	9	2	4
5	5	8	7	1	4	6	2
6	7	6	1	8	4	5	3
9	9	3	5	8	0	2	1
7	4	3	8	0	4	2	9
8	5	3	3	7	6	2	1
5	9	7	4	5	5	0	8
6	6	8	4	5	9	9	2

A12

Activities 23 – 24

NOTES FOR TEACHERS

Aim
▲ to know and use addition and subtraction number facts to 20

Notes
▲ Activities 23 and 24 are concerned with checking whether children use quick recall when solving simple number problems. Although Mastersheets A13 and A14, which are to be used in these activities, appear only to contain computational exercises it is intended that they be used to answer the type of problems outlined in the activities.

Evaluation checkpoints
▲ knows addition and subtraction facts to 20

▲ knows number facts by quick recall

▲ can total more than two numbers

▲ knows odd and even relationships when adding and subtracting

  Materials: *Mastersheet A13 (p.121)*

- At the most basic level pupils can complete Mastersheet A13 and you can observe whether or not the addition bonds are known by quick recall.

- Instead of completing all the additions on the Mastersheet the pupils could respond to questions, such as those shown below, by stating the letter(s) which correspond to the appropriate sum(s).

    - Which sums have even/odd answers?
    - Which sum has the largest total?
    - Which sums have an answer which is less than 12?

  Materials: *Mastersheet A14 (p.122)*

- At the most basic level pupils can complete Mastersheet A14 and you can observe whether the subtraction bonds are known by quick recall.

- Instead of completing all the subtractions on the Mastersheet, the children could respond to questions such as those listed below, by stating the letter(s) which correspond to the appropriate sum(s).

    - Which subtractions have even/odd answers, the largest answer, an answer of 2?

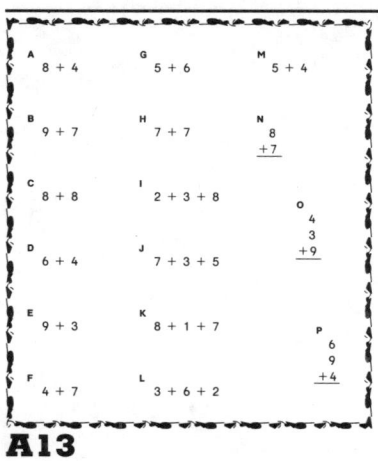

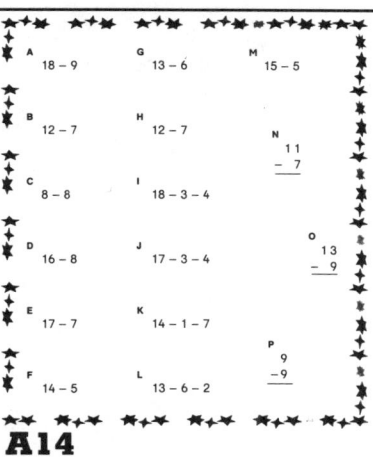

MATHS BANK: Level 3 Number Page 23

NOTES FOR TEACHERS

Activities 25 – 27

Aim
▲ to know and use addition and subtraction number facts to 20

Notes
▲ The following three activities evaluate whether children can use addition and subtraction facts to answer simple problems.

▲ Activity 25 can be used as a simple computational exercise although its intention is to evaluate whether pupils have quick recall of number facts.

▲ Activity 26 involves the pupils in solving simple addition and subtraction problems presented in a 'picture' format.

▲ Activity 27 is concerned with the link between separate number facts and addition/subtraction trios with the relationship between three related numbers explored.

Evaluation checkpoints
▲ knows addition facts to 20

▲ knows number facts by quick recall

▲ knows odd and even relationships when adding and subtracting

▲ knows addition/subtraction trios to 20

▲ knows subtraction facts to 20

▲ can total more than two numbers

25 Materials: *Mastersheet A15 (p.123)*

● At the most basic level pupils can complete the Mastersheet and you could make observations as to whether the addition and subtraction facts are known by quick recall.

● Instead of completing all the additions and subtractions on the Mastersheet the pupils could respond to questions such as those listed below, by stating the letter(s) which correspond to the appropriate 'sum(s)'.

  – Which 'sums' have even/odd answers?
  – Which 'sums' have an answer of 7?
  – Which 'sums' have answers which are less than 10?
  – Which 'sum' has the largest/smallest answer?

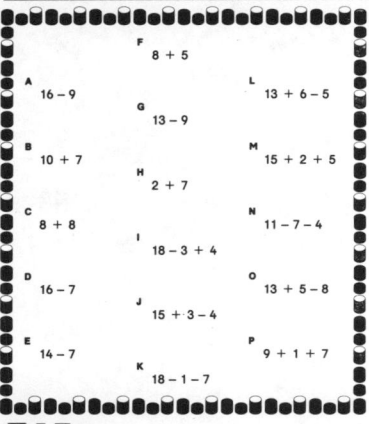

A15

Page 24 — Number — MATHS BANK: Level 3

NOTES FOR TEACHERS

Activities 25 – 27 continued

26 **Materials:** *Mastersheet A16 (p.124)*

- Mastersheet A16 contains 'picture problems' for pupils to solve using addition and subtraction facts. The fourth 'picture problem,' where they have to find a set of cards which totals 15, has more than one possible answer; check that they search for other solutions after finding one of them.

27 **Materials:** *Mastersheet A17 (p.125)*

- Mastersheet A17 has sets of three numbers which are addition/subtraction trios; for example 4, 7, 11 could be expressed as $7 + 4 = 11$, $4 + 7 = 11$, $11 - 4 = 7$ or $11 - 7 = 4$.

- The three numbers can be used to make number sentences with symbols only (such as $4 + 7 = 11$) or number sentences with symbols and words (for example, 4 more than 7 is 11). Students should be encouraged to find all the relationships between the three numbers that they can.

- Students should choose three numbers of their own which are addition/subtraction trios and then make up number sentences for each trio.

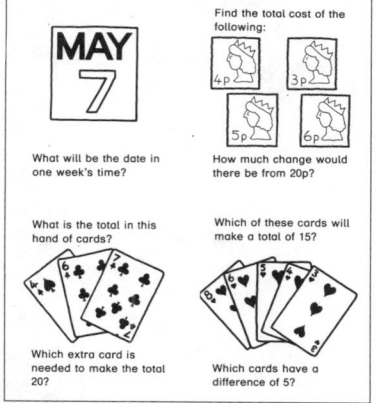

A16   A17

MATHS BANK : Level 3   Number   Page 25

Notes for Teachers

Activities 28 – 30

Aim
▲ to solve problems involving multiplication or division of whole numbers or money, using a calculator where necessary

Notes
▲ It is assumed that a calculator will be available for each of the following three activities.
▲ There are three types of problem to be solved: picture problems, word problems and practical problems.
▲ Results can be shown on a Recording Mastersheet C1, C2 or C3.
▲ Your observations can be made on Recording Mastersheet C4.

Evaluation checkpoints
▲ knows when to multiply in order to solve a problem
▲ knows when to divide in order to solve a problem
▲ can use a calculator to help solve problems
▲ can 'round off' when reading a calculator

Materials: *Mastersheet A18 (p.126)*
● Mastersheet A18 shows picture problems, with money, which will involve children in using multiplication and division skills.

Materials: *Mastersheet A19 (p.127)*
● Mastersheet A19 shows word problems which will involve the pupils in deciding whether a multiplication or division operation is needed to solve the problem. Rather than testing these particular computational skills it is assumed that a calculator will be used to calculate the actual answers. In explaining how to solve each problem you may use a range of techniques, such as describing verbally, showing which calculator touches are necessary.

● Pupils need to be involved in practical problem-solving activities where they will be using their multiplication and division skills. You could set them tasks such as:
– *Find the weight of 1000 dried peas.*
– *Find the weight of £10 worth of pennies.*
– *Approximately how many bags of potato crisps can be made from a large potato?*

● These practical problem solving activities would also contribute towards Using and applying mathematics, Level 3.

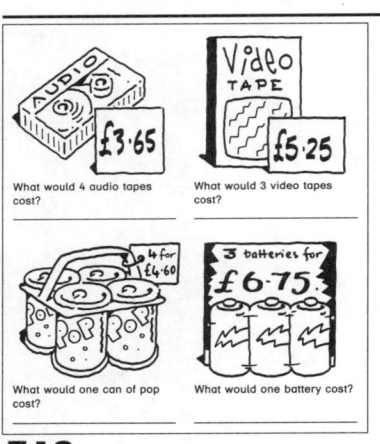
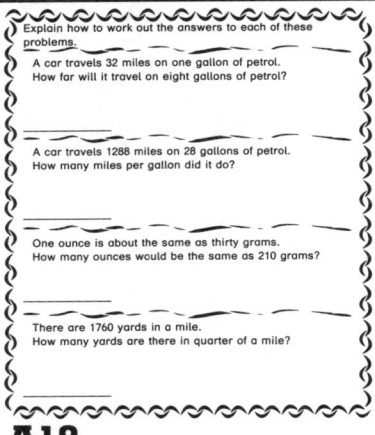

NOTES FOR TEACHERS
Activities 31 – 33

Aim
▲ to know and use multiplication facts up to 5 x 5
▲ to know all the facts in the 2, 5 and 10 multiplication tables

Notes
▲ The following activities evaluate three important aspects of multiplication:
  – commutative property, repeated addition aspect, array aspect.

Evaluation checkpoints
▲ knows all multiplication facts up to 5 x 5
▲ knows multiplication facts relating to 5
▲ knows that multiplication is commutative
▲ recognises multiplication as repeated addition
▲ can represent multiplication facts in an array
▲ knows multiplication facts relating to 2
▲ knows multiplication facts relating to 10

Materials: *Mastersheet A20 (p.128)*
● Mastersheet A20 allows you to observe whether pupils have quick recall of number facts. It also allows you to observe whether they appreciate that multiplication is commutative.

Materials: *Mastersheet C1 (p.193)*
● In order to evaluate whether pupils understand that multiplication can be shown as an array ask them to represent appropriate multiplication facts as rectangles on Recording Mastersheet C1 (cm² paper), for example:

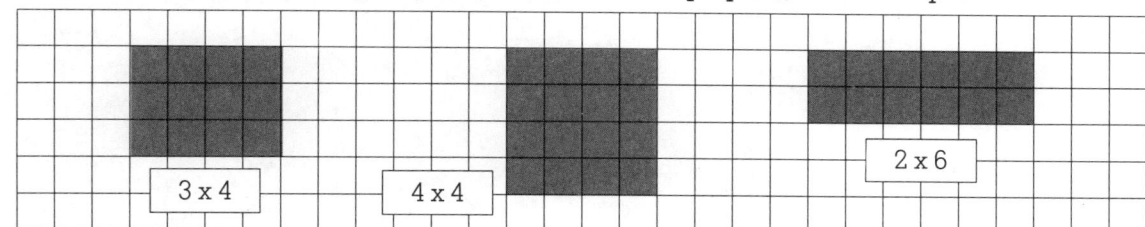

This activity is also excellent for discussing the commutative property of multiplication.

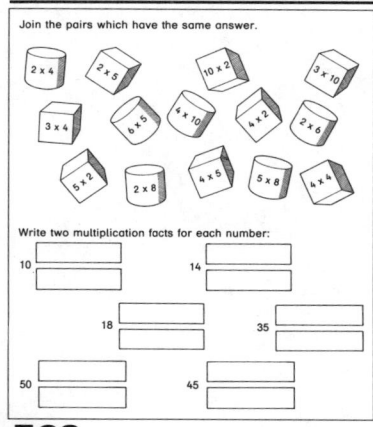

A20

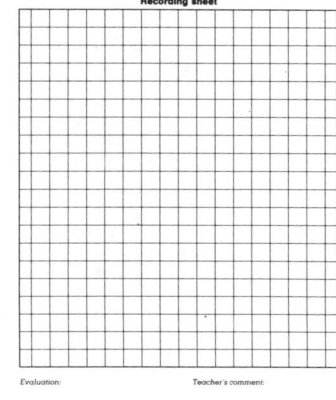

C1

MATHS BANK: Level 3 — Number — Page 27

NOTES FOR TEACHERS

Activities 31 – 33 continued

 33 **Materials:** *Mastersheet C1, C2 or C3*

- You can evaluate whether pupils appreciate that multiplication can be shown as repeated addition by asking them to write multiplication facts as addition facts and vice versa, for example:

  5 x 6 = 5 + 5 + 5 + 5 + 5 + 5,
  2 + 2 + 2 + 2 + 2 + 2 + 2 = 2 x 7

  You may wish to accept the alternative mathematical notation rather than the conventional one (for example, 4 x 2 = 2 + 2 + 2 + 2 rather than 4 x 2 = 4 + 4).

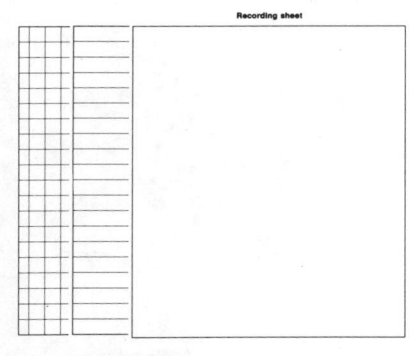

C1 C2 C3

Notes for Teachers

Activities 34 – 35

Aim
▲ to recognise that the first digit is the most important in indicating the size of a number
▲ to approximate to the nearest 10 or 100

Notes
▲ There are two aspects of estimation and approximation evaluated in the following two activities:
   - quantity (cardinal number)
   - position on a number line (positional number).
▲ These activities do not use Pupil Mastersheets. Your observations can be recorded on Recording Mastersheet C4.

Evaluation checkpoints
▲ recognises that the first digit is the most important in indicating the size of a number
▲ can approximate to the nearest 10
▲ can estimate position on a number line
▲ can approximate to the nearest 100

Materials: Mastersheet B2 (p.186)

- Masteresheet B2 should be photocopied onto thin card or paper and the individual digits cut out.
- Choose a set of four digits, for example:

- Ask pupils to make:
  - the largest 2-digit number
  - the largest 3-digit number
  - the number nearest to 350; 470; 500; 800
- The set of four numbers can be changed and the questions repeated.
- Each pupil can have a different set of four numbers and the results compared and contrasted.

B2

MATHS BANK : Level 3   Number   Page 29

NOTES FOR TEACHERS

Activities 34 – 35 continued

35 **Materials:** *strip of card*

- Use a narrow strip of card (30 cm x 5 cm approximately) onto which an elastic band is placed such that it will not slide off.

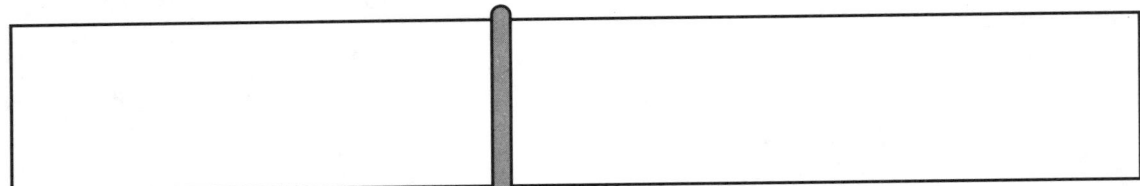

- Nominate one end of the strip as zero and the other as 100. Ask the students to slide the band to the position which shows, for example, 50, 71, 13, 79, 42 …
- Evaluate the relative accuracy of their approximations.
- The 'value' of the strip can be changed so that one end is zero and the other 1000 for students to approximate the positions of numbers within this range.
- It is possible to evaluate several students at the same time with this activity.
- The length of the card strip can be varied.

NOTES FOR TEACHERS

Activities 36 – 38

Aim
▲ to recognise that the first digit is the most important in indicating the size of a number
▲ to approximate to the nearest 10 or 100

Notes
▲ Activities 36 and 37 evaluate estimating position on number lines and Activity 38 evaluates 'rounding off' numbers using a calculator.

Evaluation checkpoints
▲ recognises that the first digit is the most important in indicating the size of a number
▲ able to approximate to the nearest 10
▲ able to approximate to the nearest 100
▲ able to estimate position on a number line

36 **Materials:** *Mastersheet A4 (p.112)*

- Nominate some numbers and ask pupils to show them on each of the number lines on Mastersheet A4.
- Evaluate the 'accuracy' of their responses.

37 **Materials:** *Mastersheet A4*

- Draw a few arrows on a copy of the Mastersheet and ask pupils which numbers they think the arrows point to, for example:

C 0 ──────────────↓─↓──↓──────── 500

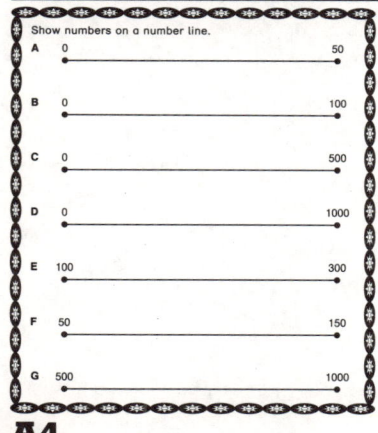

A4

Maths Bank: Level 3   Number   Page 31

NOTES FOR TEACHERS

Activities 36 – 38 continued

38 **Materials:** *a calculator and Recording Mastersheet C4 (p.196)*

- Pupils work in pairs and each has a calculator. One player enters any 2-digit number on his/her calculator provided it is not a multiple of 10. The other player 'rounds off' this number on his/her calculator to the nearest 10. The smaller number is then subtracted from the bigger one. If the result of the subtraction is 5 or less then the second player scores 5 points; if it is greater than 5 then s/he only scores 1 point. Turns are taken to go first.

- The game can be repeated with the starting number having to be a 3-digit number and the second player still having to 'round off' to the nearest 10.

- The game can be adapted so that the second player has to 'round off' to the nearest 100.

NOTES FOR TEACHERS
Activities 39 – 41

Aim
▲ to understand 'remainders' given the context of calculation, and know whether to round up or down

Notes
▲ When rounding 'remainders' up or down two considerations need to be made. In calculations it is normal to round down when the 'remainder' is less than a half and to round up when it is a half or more. In solving 'real' problems this rounding up/down rule does not always apply. It is sometimes necessary to round up/down to the next 'whole one' whatever the remainder happens to be. (For example, in practice you cannot have 2.9 children!)

Evaluation checkpoints
▲ knows when to round up
▲ knows when to round down
▲ can calculate remainders

Materials: *Use Mastersheet A21 (p.129)*

- Mastersheet A21 shows sets of eggs which have to be placed in boxes. Pupils have to calculate the number of boxes needed to hold the eggs. With each calculation one box will not be completely filled.

- Pupils can also calculate how many more eggs are needed in order to fill up each partly filled box.

Materials: *Recording Mastersheet C1, C2 or C3 (pp.193 – 5)*

- Pupils can be given word problems which will involve them in rounding up/down. For example:

    How many 30cl bottles can be filled from: 1 litre, 2 litres, 3 litres?

    How many 30p ices can be bought for: £1, £2, £3?

    How many 40cm lengths can be cut from a plank of the following lengths: 1 metre, 2 metres, 3 metres?

    How many boxes are needed to hold 46 tins if there are 10 tins to a box?

- Calculations can be shown on Mastersheet C1, C2 or C3.

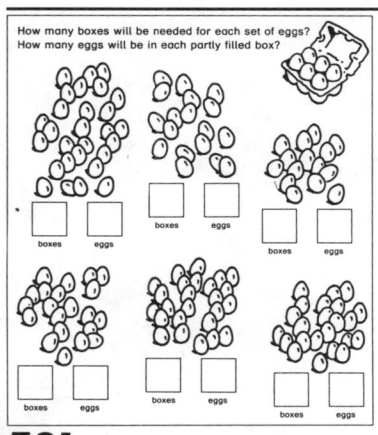

A21

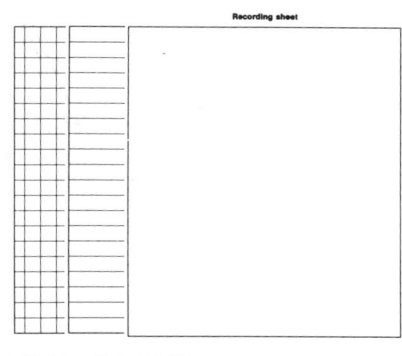

C1 C2 C3

MATHS BANK: Level 3   Number   Page 33

NOTES FOR TEACHERS

Activities 39 – 41 continued

41 **Materials:** Mastersheet C1, C2 or C3

- Pupils can be given mental calculations which involve them in using and understanding remainders, for example:
  - *I divide a number by 4 and the remainder is 2. What could the number be?*
  - *Which numbers when divided by 7 leave a remainder of: 1, 4, 5?*
  - *What are the remainders when I divide 50 by: 9, 8, 7, 6, 5, 4, 3, 2?*
  - *I have a remainder of 7. What could I have divided by?*

- Answers can either be oral or be recorded onto Mastersheet C1, C2 or C3.

C1 C2 C3

NOTES FOR TEACHERS
Activities 42 – 43

Aim
▲ to explain number patterns and predict subsequent numbers where appropriate

Notes
▲ Activities 42 and 43 consider sequences and pupils' ability to predict what will happen in those sequences. There are two levels of understanding which can be evaluated:
- the ability to predict the subsequent numbers or items in a sequence
- the ability to predict what will happen in any position in the sequence (i.e. predict the 'n' th term of a sequence).

The ability to do the latter requires some considerable insight into sequences by pupils and is very challenging.

Evaluation checkpoints
▲ able to predict the next term in a simple sequence
▲ able to predict the 'n' th term in a simple sequence

Materials: *Multilink cubes and Mastersheet C1, C2 or C3 (pp.193 – 5)*

- As a starting point pupils should be given sticks of cubes which have a simple sequence of colours, for example:

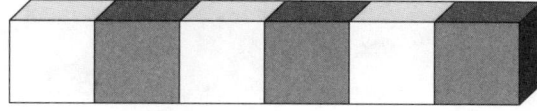 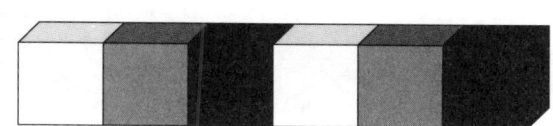

The complexity of the starting sticks is a matter of your discretion.
- Ask pupils whether they can predict the colour of, for example, the tenth cube, fifteenth cube, and so on.
- Their predictions can be checked by continuing the pattern for each stick.
- Both Multilink cubes and prisms can also be used as starting points for pupils to predict colour and shape.
- The patterns and predictions can be copied onto Recording Mastersheet C1, C2 or C3.

C1 C2 C3

MATHS BANK : Level 3 Number/Algebra

NOTES FOR TEACHERS

Activities 42 – 43 continued

Materials: *Mastersheet A22 (p.130)*

- Mastersheet A22 has a collection of sequences for children to complete. Some of the sequences are repeating patterns whilst others are part of a number pattern such as the five times table.

- Pupils are asked to record the next two 'terms' in each sequence and also to predict the tenth term.

What are the next two numbers in each pattern?
Try to predict which number will come in the tenth position.

                                                      10th number

1 2 3 1 2 3 _ _ ... ☐

5 10 15 20 25 _ _ ... ☐

1 2 1 3 1 4 1 _ _ ... ☐

13 23 33 43 53 _ _ ... ☐

100 96 92 88 84 _ _ ... ☐

1 5 2 10 3 15 _ _ ... ☐

A22

Page 36   Number/Algebra   MATHS BANK: Level 3

Notes for Teachers

Activities 44 – 45

Aim
▲ to explain number patterns and predict subsequent numbers where appropriate

Notes
▲ The following activities use '100 grids' on Mastersheets A23 and A24 for pupils to look for pattern. The normal '100 grid' is not the only one used, as this often restricts pupils' ability to look for pattern. Instead, the numbers are arranged in a variety of ways on the grids, as follows:

   Mastersheet A23   Grid A is a normal '100 grid'.
                             Grid B has the numbers 0 – 99 arranged in a zigzag pattern, rather like a snakes and ladders board.

   Mastersheet A24   Grid C has the numbers arranged in a spiral going inwards to the centre.
                             Grid D has the numbers arranged in a spiral going from the centre outwards in an anticlockwise direction.

Not all the numbers are written on each grid. A few are there to act as guide numbers to assist the children in spotting the patterns.

▲ The activities can be conducted with children working as individuals within groups.

▲ For each activity any of the four grids may be used, or each activity can be repeated on each grid.

Evaluation checkpoints
▲ able to describe number patterns on a grid
▲ able to predict where numbers will go on a number grid
▲ able to recognise 'special' numbers such as odd, even, square, multiples
▲ finds positions of numbers by counting
▲ finds positions of numbers by looking for patterns

Materials: *Mastersheet A23 (p.131) and/or Mastersheet A24 (p.132)*

● Choose which grid(s) you wish the pupils to work on.

● Give them random numbers to place on their grids and observe whether they find the positions of the numbers by counting from the start, by counting on/back from existing numbers or by looking for patterns.

● Allow the pupils to describe the pattern that the numbers make on each grid.

● Note whether pupils need to write in all the missing numbers on each grid or whether they can find their way about the grids with just a few numbers showing.

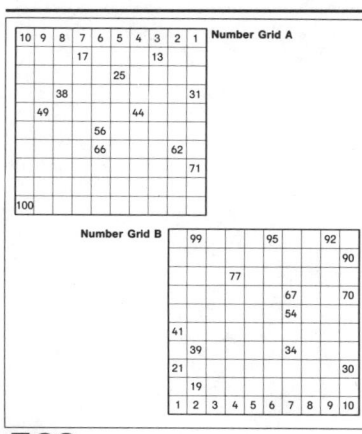

A23

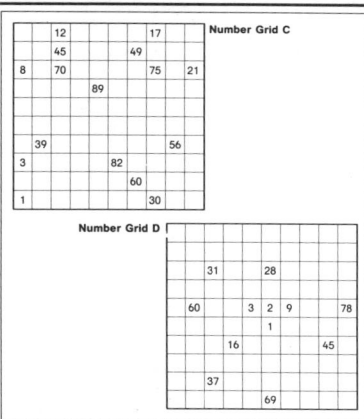

A24

Maths Bank : Level 3   Number/Algebra   Page 37

NOTES FOR TEACHERS

Activities 44 – 45 continued

45 **Materials:** *Mastersheet A23 and/or Mastersheet A24*

- Choose which grid(s) you wish the pupils to work on.
- Ask them to place on the grid(s) numbers with a specific property, such as:
  - all numbers which have an 8 in them
  - multiples of 5
  - even numbers

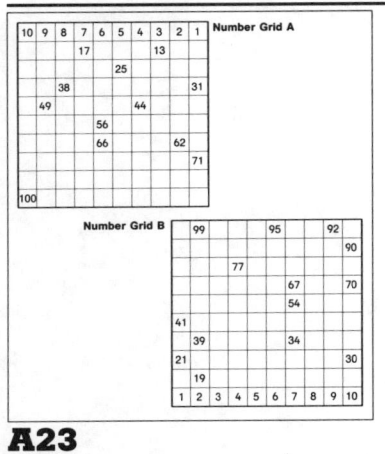

A23

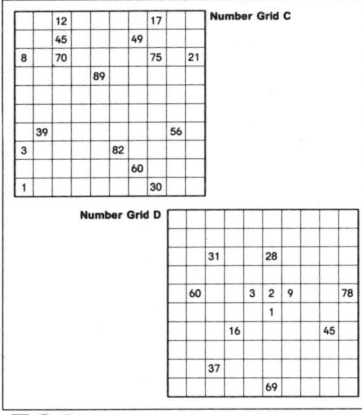

A24

NOTES FOR TEACHERS

Activities 46 – 48

Aim
▲ to find number patterns and equivalent forms of 2-digit numbers and use these to perform mental calculations

Notes
▲ The following three activities are concerned with evaluating possible strategies that pupils may use in order to solve calculations mentally. The first activity considers equivalent forms of writing 2-digit numbers (such as 59 = 50 + 9 or 60 – 1), the second evaluates whether pupils can perform simple mental activities and the third considers the role of counting on/back in performing mental calculations.

Evaluation checkpoints
▲ can express 2-digit numbers in equivalent forms
▲ can calculate mentally using a variety of techniques
▲ can use counting techniques to add and subtract mentally

Materials: *Mastersheet A25 (p.133)*

● In Mastersheet A25 pupils are asked to write 2-digit numbers in equivalent forms. Some of the equivalent forms are more useful than others when performing mental calculations: this can lead to some discussion on 'useful' forms (for instance when adding 99 it is quicker to add 100 then subtract 1).

● Pupils should be given mental calculations to perform. Your observations and comments can be recorded on Mastersheet C4.

● The types of mental calculations can include:
  – adding 9, 19, 29 … to 2-digit numbers
  – subtracting 9, 19, 29 … from 2-digit numbers
  – adding two 2-digit numbers when no 'exchanging' is involved (such as 34 + 55)
  – adding two 2-digit numbers when 'exchanging' is involved (such as 26 + 35)
  – subtracting two 2-digit numbers when no 'exchanging' is involved (such as 87 – 54)
  – subtracting two 2-digit numbers when 'exchanging' is involved (such as 61 – 35)
  – doubling 2-digit numbers
  – halving 2-digit numbers

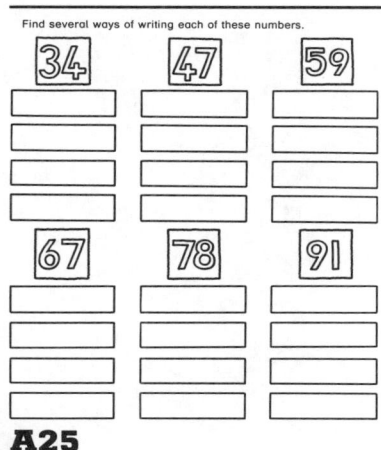

A25

MATHS BANK: Level 3   Number/Algebra   Page 39

NOTES FOR TEACHERS

Activities 46 – 48 continued

48
- Recognising when to 'count on' or 'count back' rather than use more complex techniques is an important 'skill' which may aid mental calculation. Usually these two counting on/counting back techniques come to the fore during subtractions when either:
  - the two numbers are 'close' numbers (such as 30 – 28, 58 – 54)
  - the number being subtracted is small (such as 30 – 2, 76 – 4)
- Give pupils subtractions to solve mentally where the numbers are 'close' and where one of the numbers is small.
- Evaluate whether students use a mental counting on technique when subtracting 'close numbers' and a mental counting back technique when subtracting small numbers.
- Observations can be recorded on Mastersheet C4.

Notes for Teachers

Activities 49 – 51

Aim
▲ to recognise whole numbers which are exactly divisible by 2, 5 and 10

Notes
▲ Activity 49 uses digit cards to generate 3-digit numbers randomly and Activities 50 and 51 use dice to generate 2-digit numbers randomly. What is being evaluated here is pupils' ability to recognise numbers which are divisible by 2, 5 or 10 irrespective of the size of number.

Evaluation checkpoints
▲ recognise numbers which are divisible by 2
▲ recognise numbers which are divisible by 5
▲ recognise numbers which are divisible by 10
▲ recognise that numbers which are divisible by 10 are also divisible by 2 and 5
▲ able to sort numbers onto Venn and Carroll diagrams

Materials: *Mastersheet A26 (p.134) and Mastersheet B2 (p.186)*

- Pupils play this game in small groups.
- Mastersheet B2 needs to be copied and the individual digits cut out.
- The digit cards are shuffled and placed face down between the players who each have a copy of Mastersheet A26.
- The first player shuffles the digit cards and then looks at the top card. S/he decides which of the three spaces on the Mastersheet to place the card: this is repeated for two more cards so that eventually the player has a 3-digit number. Then, if the 3-digit number is divisible by:
  – 2, but not 10, score 1 point
  – 5, but not 10, score 2 points
  – 10, score 3 points
- Players take turns to make 3-digit numbers in this way.
- The game is over either after an agreed number of rounds or upon reaching an agreed total.

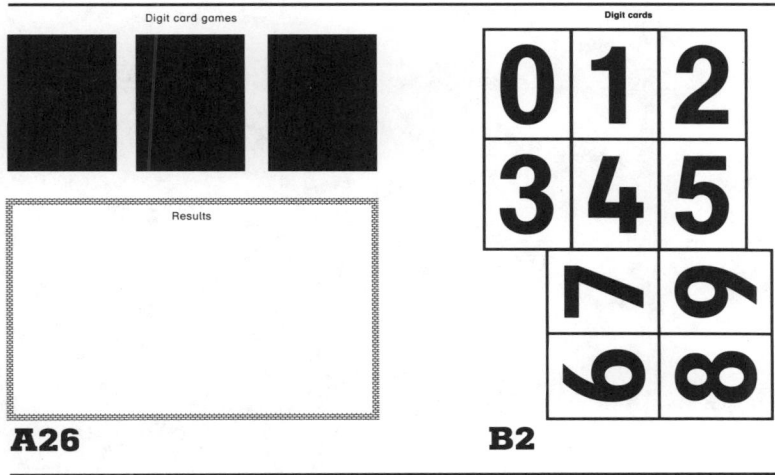

MATHS BANK : Level 3   Number/Algebra   Page 41

NOTES FOR TEACHERS

Activities 49 – 51 continued

- The numbers made by each player can be recorded on the Mastersheet in the space provided.
- Observation should make it clear which pupils immediately recognise numbers that are divisible by 2, 5 or 10.

50 **Materials:** *Mastersheet A27 (p.135) and two dice*

51 **Materials:** *Mastersheet A28 (p.136) and two dice*

- In both activities two dice are rolled and placed side by side to generate a 2-digit number. Pupils can choose in which order to use the dice. Several numbers are generated in this way.
- Pupils then have to decide whereabouts the numbers have to be written:
  - on the Venn diagram (Mastersheet A27, Activity 50)
  - on the Carroll diagram (Mastersheet A28, Activity 51)

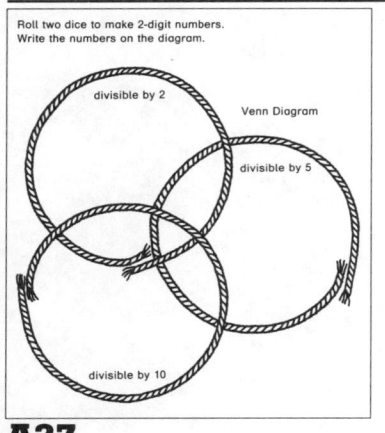

A27

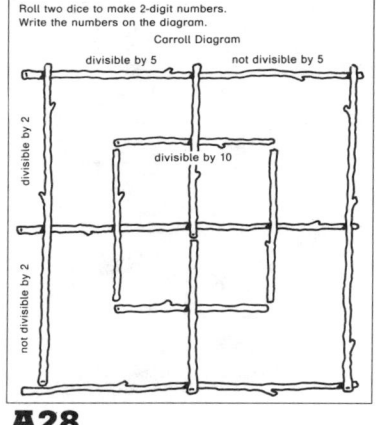

A28

NOTES FOR TEACHERS
Activities 52 – 54

Aim
▲ to deal with inputs to and outputs from simple function machines

Notes
▲ Three aspects of using a function machine are explored in the following three activities:
- Activity 52 considers the output when the input and function are shown
- Activity 53 considers the input when the output and function are shown
- Activity 54 considers the function when the input and output are shown

▲ When a list of numbers is shown entering a machine consideration needs to be given as to the order in which they leave it, for example:

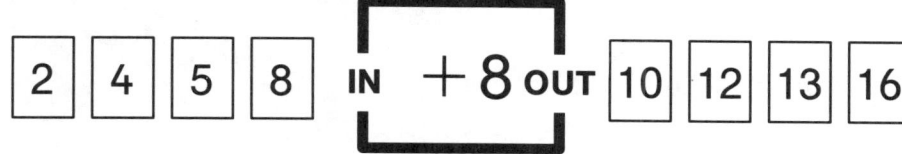

Evaluation checkpoints
▲ can calculate outputs from function machines
▲ can calculate inputs into a function machine
▲ can work out the function of a machine

 Materials: *Mastersheet A29 (p.137)*

● Mastersheet A29 shows function machines with the input and function given. Pupils have to calculate the output for each machine.

● Some of the machines are slightly more complex than others, involving two operations within the one function (for example, x 2 + 1).

 Materials: *Mastersheet A30 (p.138)*

● Mastersheet A30 shows function machines with the output and function given. Pupils have to calculate the inputs for each machine.

● This activity evaluates whether the children understand inverse operations such as addition being the inverse of subtraction.

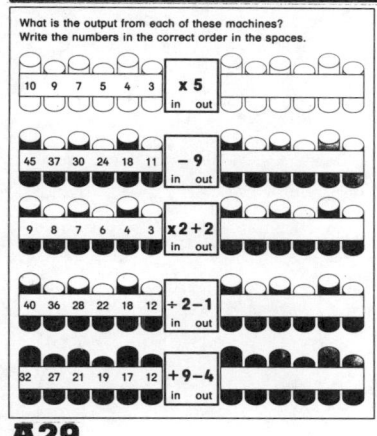
A29

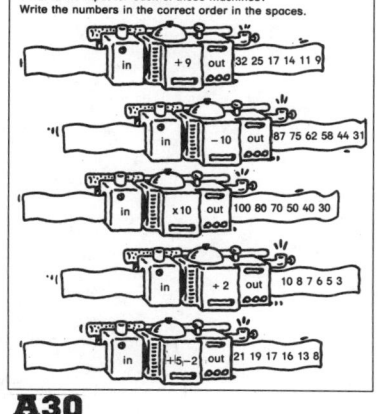
A30

MATHS BANK: Level 3   Algebra   Page 43

NOTES FOR TEACHERS

Activities 52 – 54 continued

54 **Materials:** *Mastersheet A31 (p.139)*

- Mastersheet A31 shows function machines with both the input and output given. Pupils have to work out the function of the machine.

- The final two machines have only one input and one output shown, which means that there are many possible answers. Encourage pupils to explore alternative functions. Once they have decided upon a function they can add more inputs and outputs to their machines.

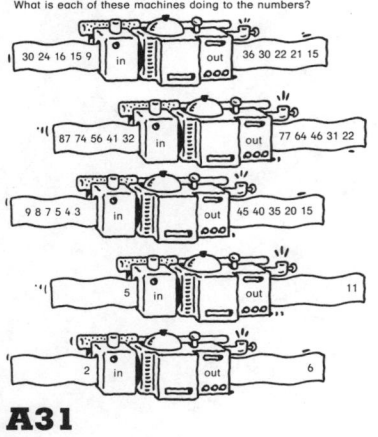

A31

Algebra

Measures

Introduction

The Measures activities are grouped as follows:

- use of a wider range of metric units
- choice and use of appropriate units and instruments in a variety of situations, interpreting numbers on a range of measuring instruments
- making estimates based on familiar units

The grouping of the activities is shown overleaf, while their relationship to the National Curriculum statements of attainment is shown on pages 207 – 8.

- There is a subtle difference between measuring the length of an object and measuring the distance between two points. Both these aspects are included in the activities in this chapter.

- Whether the word 'mass' or 'weight' is used during these activities is a matter of personal preference. Although, strictly speaking, 'mass' is the correct term to use in many of the activities, the word 'weight' is more commonly used and understood.

- When recording measures, many pupils may well use decimal notation, especially in length. It is worth noting that the decimal point used in this way is acting as a 'separator' between two units (such as between pounds and pence) rather than as a true decimal. The relationship between two units is appropriate to Measures: Level 4 although many pupils will demonstrate an understanding whilst engaged in these Level 3 activities.

- The practical measuring activities offer the opportunity to estimate before measuring. It is worth encouraging pupils to estimate and measure each item in turn rather than estimate all items to be measured before measuring them. The latter technique does not allow for improvement of estimation skills. If a numerical calculation is made between the estimation and measurement and this result called 'error' it can have an adverse effect upon pupils' estimating as they may not realise that quite a large numerical 'error' may in fact be a very good estimate. Much discussion needs to take place as to what are 'good' estimates.

- When ordering activities are taking place the opportunity exists to assess whether pupils understand the notion of transitivity, for example:

  A is heavier than B, B is heavier than C, therefore A is heavier than C

- The weighing activities include two aspects of weight: weighing an object to find how heavy it is and balancing against a known weight to find how much is needed to match that weight. The ability to interpret the dial on weighing scales and systematically to add weights to a balance are both evaluated.

- As both cl and dl are in fairly common usage the opportunity exists to evaluate the use of both units.

Pages 47 – 60 may be photocopied

Activities 55 – 76

The Measures activities are grouped as follows:

Activities Statements

55 – 57 ⎰ use a wider range of metric units
64 – 66 ⎱ make estimates based on familiar units

58 – 63   use a wider range of metric units

   choose and use appropriate units and instruments in a variety of situations, interpreting numbers on a range of measuring instruments

   make estimates based on familiar units

67 – 69   choose and use appropriate units and instruments in a variety of situations, interpreting numbers on a range of measuring instruments

70 – 76   make estimates based on familiar units

NOTES FOR TEACHERS

Activities 55 – 57

Aim
▲ to use a wider range of metric units
▲ to make sensible estimates involving cm

Notes
▲ The following activities are concerned with pupils measuring and recording objects and distances in centimetres using a metre stick as a 'long ruler'.

▲ It is common to find pupils who have only used a metre stick to measure things which are longer than a metre. These activities include measuring objects which are longer and shorter than a metre.

▲ When pupils are using a table to show the results of their measurements check that they estimate and measure each item in turn rather than estimate a whole range of items and then measure them, otherwise trial and improvement 'skills' will not develop.

Evaluation checkpoints
▲ able to measure length accurately
▲ able to read and use a metre stick
▲ able to estimate length sensibly

55 56 *Materials: Mastersheet C5 (p.197) and a metre stick*

- In both activities pupils measure a whole range of distances and lengths with a metre stick where the item being measured is:
  - **less than** a metre (Activity 55)
  - **more than** a metre (Activity 56)

- The items being measured can be predetermined by you and entered onto a copy of Mastersheet C5 or be a free choice on the part of the pupils.

- Check estimation skills on one or two of the items being measured.

- Discuss whether the items being measured are to be recorded:
  - to the nearest centimetre (or to the millimetre) marks, if applicable (Activity 55)
  - as centimetres, metres and centimetres, or metre notation (Activity 56)

Table of measurements

What was measured	Unit used	Estimate	Measurement

Evaluation: Teacher's comment:

C5

MATHS BANK: Level 3   Measures

NOTES FOR TEACHERS

Activities 55 – 57 continued

57 **Materials:** *Mastersheet C1, C2 or C3 (pp.193 – 5) a metre stick and some counters*

- Pupils explore how far they can flip a counter, as in a game of Tiddlywinks. They will have to keep note of the starting point.
- They should have a specified number of attempts and see which attempt is the best.
- The results of their experiment can be shown in a rich variety of ways, for example:
  - in a table
  - by diagrams
  - in a chart
  - direct representation shown on the actual paper
- Results should be measured with the metre stick.

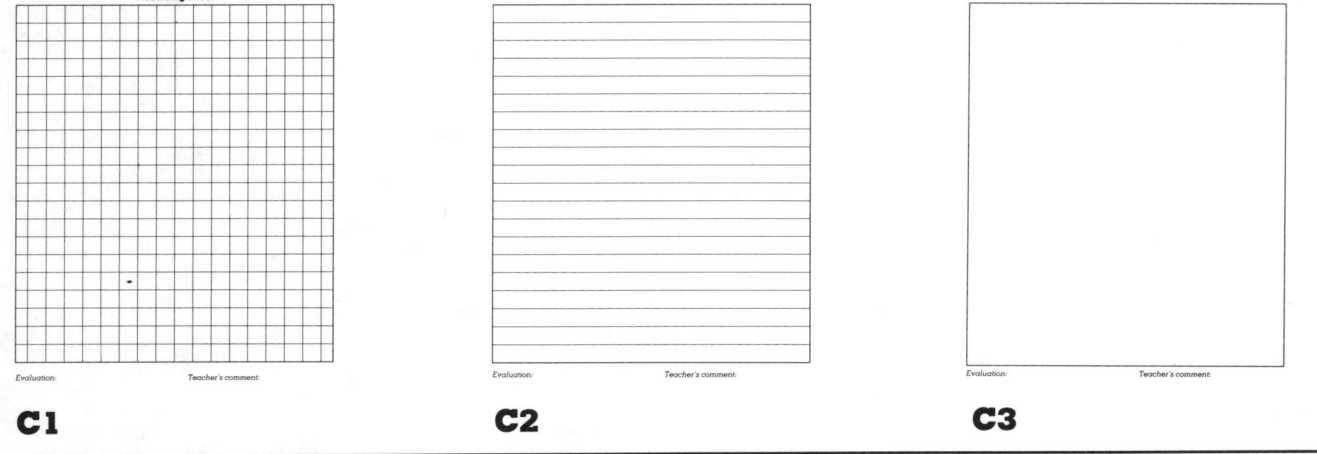

Page 48   Measures   MATHS BANK: Level 3

NOTES FOR TEACHERS

Activities 58 – 60

Aim
▲ to use a wider range of metric units
▲ to use a balance efficiently
▲ to use and read weighing scales appropriately
▲ to make sensible estimates based on grams

Notes
▲ The following activities are concerned with weighing an item using a) scales and b) balances: the former relies upon the ability to interpret the dial on the scales and the latter expects that a systematic approach be used when adding the weights to the balance. Both are important skills.

▲ The opportunity exists for you to evaluate whether transitivity of weight is understood (i.e. if A is heavier than B, and B is heavier than C, then A must be heavier than C).

Evaluation checkpoints
▲ can weigh appropriately with balances
▲ able to estimate sensibly
▲ can weigh appropriately with scales
▲ understands transitivity of weight

58 **Materials:** *Mastersheet C5 (p.197), a balance, metric weights*

59 **Materials:** *Mastersheet C5 and scales*

- Pupils weigh a whole range of items with:
  - a balance where the item being measured is less than a kilogram (Activity 58)
  - scales where the item being measured is more than a kilogram (Activity 59).
- The items being weighed can be predetermined by you and entered onto a copy of Mastersheet C5 or be a free choice on the part of the pupils.
- Discuss whether the items being measured are to be recorded to the gram or as sensible approximations.
- In Activity 59, check that the numbers on the dial of the scales are being interpreted appropriately.

C5

MATHS BANK: Level 3   Measures   Page 49

NOTES FOR TEACHERS

Activities 58 – 60 continued

60 Materials: *Mastersheet C1, C2 or C3 (p.193 – 5) and a set of 5 or 6 items to weigh*

- The set of items should be fairly close in weight – similar boxes with varying amounts of sand in them are ideal.
- Pupils should be set the task of ordering the set of items according to their weight using either scales or balances to help in the task.
- Pupils' understanding of the principle of transitivity can be assessed.

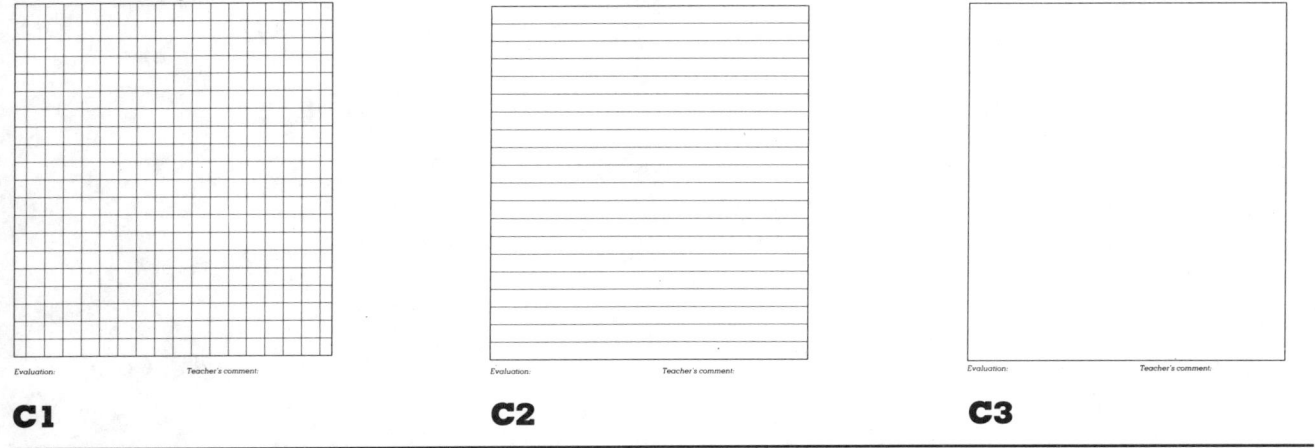

NOTES FOR TEACHERS

Activities 61 – 63

Aim
▲ to use a wider range of metric units
▲ to use a balance efficiently
▲ to use and read weighing scales appropriately
▲ to make estimates based on grams and kilograms

Notes
▲ The following activities include two aspects of weighing: firstly finding the weight of an 'object' (such as weighing someone) and secondly, finding out how much of a substance (such as potatoes or sugar) is equivalent to a standard weight (such as $\frac{1}{2}$ kg).

▲ The activities also offer the opportunity to assess whether conservation of weight is understood.

▲ Scales and balances should both be used and the different skills associated with each (reading dials and adding weights systematically) evaluated.

▲ Both weighing in kilograms and weighing in grams are included in these activities but it is not expected that pupils will explore the equivalence between the two.

Evaluation checkpoints
▲ can weigh appropriately with balances
▲ able to estimate sensibly
▲ can weigh appropriately with scales
▲ understands conservation of weight

61 *Materials:* Mastersheet C5 (p.197) and a set of bathroom scales

● Pupils find the weights of several fellow pupils. They should estimate each person's weight before checking the estimate and entering it on the Mastersheet.

● Check that the readings on the scales are being interpreted sensibly.

C5

MATHS BANK: Level 3 Measures Page 51

NOTES FOR TEACHERS

Activities 61 – 63 continued

62 **Materials:** *Mastersheet C1, C2 or C3 (pp.193 – 5)*
- Either scales or balances can be used in this activity.
- Pupils find what 30g 'heaps' of the following look like:
  sand, polystyrene bits, rice, paper, dried peas, pasta, paperclips
- The various 30g 'heaps' can be compared: (largest, smallest)
- Whether conservation of weight is understood can be evaluated.

63 **Materials:** *Mastersheet C5*
- Either scales or balances can be used in this activity.
- Pupils use scales to weigh a whole range of items which are each more than a kilogram.
- The items being weighed can be predetermined by you and entered onto a copy of Mastersheet C5 or be a free choice on the part of the pupils.
- Discuss whether each item is to be weighed to the nearest kilogram or whether part kilograms are to be used.
- Check estimation skills on one or two of the items being weighed.
- Check that the numbers on the dial of the scales are being interpreted appropriately or that the weights are being added systematically.

C1 C2 C3   **C5**

Page 52   Measures   MATHS BANK: Level 3

NOTES FOR TEACHERS
Activities 64 – 66

Aim
▲ to use a wider range of metric units
▲ to make sensible estimates involving ml

Notes
▲ The following three activities are concerned with pupils measuring and recording the capacity of containers using ml, cl and litres. Centilitres have been included as they are now in fairly common usage.

▲ When pupils are using a table to show the results of their measurements check that they estimate and find the capacity of each container in turn. They should not estimate the capacities of a whole range of containers before measuring them individually, otherwise trial and improvement 'skills' will not develop.

Evaluation checkpoints
▲ can measure capacity accurately in: ml cl litres
▲ can read a measuring jug/cylinder
▲ can estimate sensibly

Materials: *Mastersheet C5 (p.197) and a measuring jug or cylinder*

- Pupils measure the capacities of a wide range of containers using a measuring jug/cylinder, where each container being measured is less than a litre.
- The containers being measured can be predetermined by you and entered onto a copy of Mastersheet C5 or be a free choice on the part of the pupils.
- Check estimation skills on one or two of the containers being measured.
- Discuss whether the items being measured are to be recorded to the nearest millilitre or to the nearest centilitre.

Materials: *Mastersheet C5 and a litre container*

- Using a litre container pupils find the capacities of a whole range of 'large' containers (such as buckets, bowls, kettles) where each one being measured is more than a litre.
- The containers being measured can be predetermined by you and entered onto a copy of Mastersheet C5 or be a free choice on the part of the pupils.

Table of measurements

What was measured	Unit used	Estimate	Measurement

Evaluation: Teacher's comment:

C5

MATHS BANK : Level 3 Measures Page 53

NOTES FOR TEACHERS

Activities 64 – 66 continued

- Check estimation skills on one or two of the containers being measured.
- Discuss whether the containers being measured are to be recorded to the nearest litre or whether some approximations are to be used such as 'nearly four litres' and 'just over five litres'.

66 **Materials:** *Mastersheet C5 and a litre jug/cylinder which will measure cl*

- Pupils find the capacities of a range of containers using the centilitre as the unit of measurement.
- The containers being measured can be predetermined by you and entered onto a copy of Mastersheet C5 or be a free choice on the part of the pupils.
- Check estimation skills on one or two of the containers being measured.

Table of measurements

What was measured	Unit used	Estimate	Measurement

Evaluation: Teacher's comment:

C5

NOTES FOR TEACHERS
Activities 67 – 69

Aim
▲ to choose and use appropriate units and instruments in a variety of situations
▲ to interpret numbers on a range of measuring instruments

Notes
▲ Three aspects of measurement can be assessed during the following activities:
  - the ability to choose an appropriate instrument for the measuring task in hand
  - choosing an appropriate unit of measurement to use
  - interpreting the numbers on the measuring instrument.

▲ A rich variety of measuring instruments should be available from which pupils can select. These should include items such as:

rulers, tapes, bow calipers, sliding calipers, feeler gauges, weighing scales, balances, spring balances, personal scales, measuring jugs, measuring cylinders, medicine spoons, clocks, watches (digital and analogue), stop watches, tockers, sand timers, thermometers.

▲ When reading measuring instruments, many pupils will display an appreciation of the relationship between the units and record the measurement accordingly. This understanding can be recorded on the appropriate pupil Mastersheet.

Evaluation checkpoints
▲ chooses appropriate measuring instrument for task in hand
▲ can interpret numbers on a wide range of measuring instruments
▲ understands appropriate units of measurement

Materials: *Mastersheet A32 (p.140) and a range of measuring instruments*
- The Mastersheet can be completed over a period of time.
- Pupils should select for themselves which instruments to use for each measuring task.
- For some measuring tasks one of several instruments would be appropriate to use.
- Check that pupils enter the units of measurement used for each item.

Measure each of these items:

Item to be measured	Instrument used	Estimate	Measurement
Perimeter of wastepaper container			
Gap under a door			
Length of playground			
Your hand span			
Diameter of a tin			
Weight of a house brick			
Weight of 30 Multilink cubes			
Temperature of water from the cold tap			
Temperature of the classroom			
Capacity of a cup			
Capacity of a jug			
Time to write name and address neatly			

A32

MATHS BANK: Level 3   Measures   Page 55

NOTES FOR TEACHERS

Activities 67 – 69 continued

68 **Materials:** *Mastersheet A33 (p.141)*

- Pupils are asked to record on their Mastersheets the readings shown in each picture.
- Check that each unit of measurement is recorded appropriately.
- The car speedometer shows two pieces of information: distance and speed.
- When the instruments record a measurement which is between two numbered divisions some pupils may record 'to the nearest' reading whilst others may record the reading as accurately as possible. Understanding the relationship between two units is in Measures: Level 4.

69 **Materials:** *Mastersheet A34 (p.142)*

- Pupils record the missing unit of measurement which goes with each picture.
- All the units are metric.

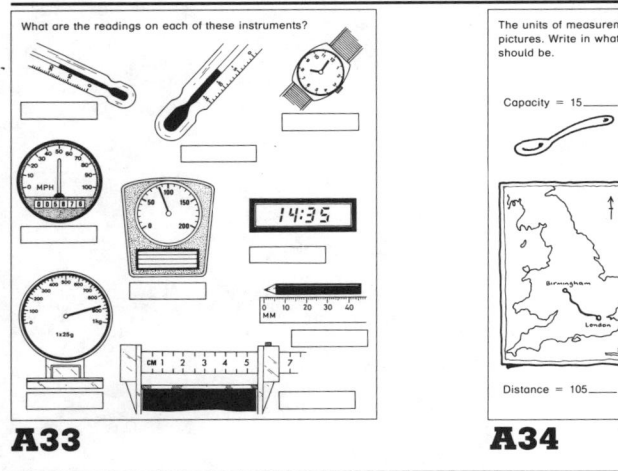

A33

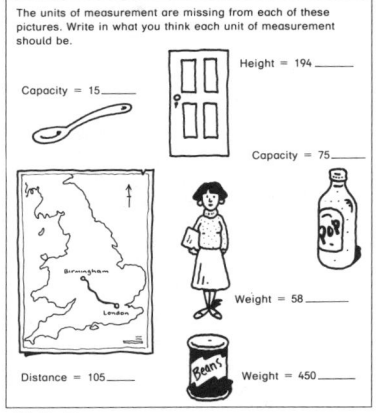

A34

NOTES FOR TEACHERS

Activities 70 – 73

Aim
▲ to make estimates based on familiar units

Notes
▲ The opportunity to estimate whilst being involved in measuring tasks is included in many of the previous activities (Activities 55–67)

Evaluation checkpoints
▲ can make sensible estimates in: length weight capacity

 Materials: strip of card 30cm x 4cm with elastic band attached, Mastersheet C1, C2 or C3 (pp.193 – 5) and a ruler

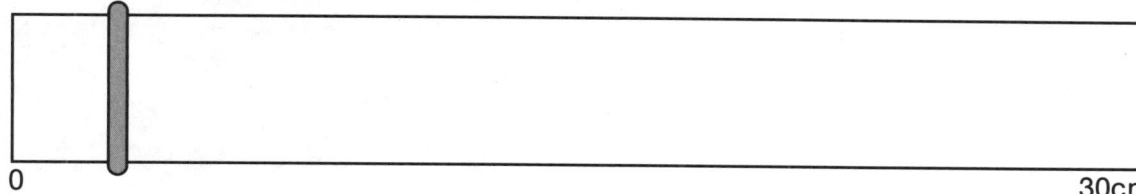

0   30cm

- Pupils work in pairs with one card strip between them.
- Turns are taken to slide the elastic band along the strip to any position. The other pupil has to estimate the distance of the band from the left hand edge. The estimate is then checked with a ruler.
- Estimates and measurements can be in cm or mm.
- The estimates and actual measurements are recorded on each individual's Mastersheet.
- Discuss what makes a 'good' estimate.
- The length of the card strip can of course be varied.

 Materials: a metre stick which has a blank side and an elastic band, and Mastersheet C1, C2 or C3

- An elastic band is placed on the metre stick.
- The activity is now conducted as for Activity 70.

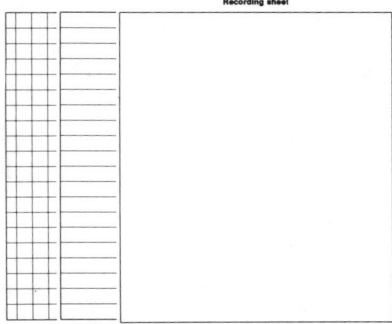

C1 C2 C3

MATHS BANK: Level 3   Measures   Page 57

NOTES FOR TEACHERS

Activities 70 – 73 continued

 72 **Materials:** *a range of items for estimating weight and Mastersheet C1, C2 or C3*

- Pupils work in pairs taking turns to choose an item, estimate its weight then check the estimate.
- The estimates and actual measurements are recorded on each individual's Mastersheet.
- Discuss what makes a 'good' estimate.

 73 **Materials:** *a range of containers for estimating capacity and Mastersheet C1, C2 or C3*

- Pupils work in pairs taking turns to choose a container, estimate its capacity then check the estimate.
- The activity is then conducted as for Activity 72.

C1 C2 C3

NOTES FOR TEACHERS

Activities 74 – 76

Aim
▲ to make estimates based on time

Notes
▲ Estimating time and the concept of time are difficult areas to understand because time is not 'visible' and the apparent passage of time can depend upon what you are doing and whether the task is enjoyable. The notion of a 'long time' is often subjective.

Evaluation checkpoints
▲ can estimate short periods of time

Materials: *Mastersheet C4 (p.196)*

- Mark two lines some distance apart on the playground, hall or classroom floor.
- Pupils start from one line and have to walk to the other in the time you state (such as 30 seconds).
- Watches should be removed before this activity.
- Observe which children cross the line within a sensible approximation of the allotted time.
- The 'walking time' should then be varied.

Materials: *Mastersheet C1, C2 or C3 (pp.193 – 5)*

- Pupils have to estimate how long it will take them to perform a simple task set by you for example:
  - *Thread a nominated number of beads on a lace*
  - *Get changed ready for PE or games*
  - *Lace a shoe*
  - *Walk across the playground.*
- Their estimate is recorded, then the task is undertaken, timed, and compared with the estimate.
- Discuss what are 'good' estimates.

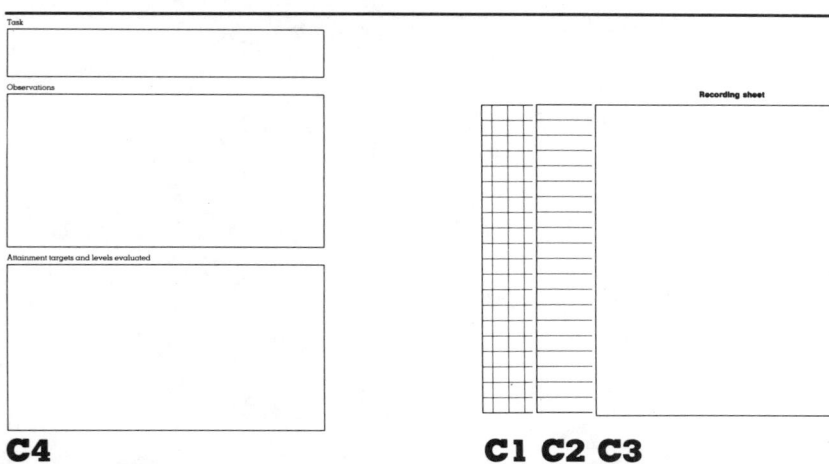

C4 **C1 C2 C3**

MATHS BANK : Level 3   Measures   Page 59

NOTES FOR TEACHERS

Activities 74 – 76 continued

Materials: Mastersheet C1, C2 or C3

- Pupils have to estimate the time between two 'sounds' such as between two claps of your hands.
- The estimates are recorded by the pupils on their Mastersheets.
- Vary the time between the start and finish 'sounds' from a few seconds to a few minutes: pupils may be working on another activity (such as PE) between the two 'sounds'.

C1 C2 C3

Shape and Space

Introduction

The Shape and space activities assess whether children are able to:

- sort 2-D and 3-D shapes in different ways and give reasons for each method of sorting

- recognise the (reflective) symmetry in a variety of shapes in 2 and 3 dimensions

- understand eight points of the compass; use clockwise and anti-clockwise appropriately

The grouping of the activities is shown overleaf, while their relationship to the National Curriculum statements of attainment is shown on pages 207 – 8.

- When pupils are sorting shapes in different ways some of the criteria for sorting might include:
    - number of sides/faces
    - angle properties
    - whether they are symmetrical
    - whether they tessellate
    - parallel/non parallel sides
    - straight/curved faces.

The pupils should be encouraged to explore a rich variety of reasons for sorting a collection of shapes. Sorting the same collection for different criteria helps pupils to look for different ways to sort.

- When giving their own reasons for sorting shapes pupils may well express criteria referred to in several Levels of the National Curriculum.

- It is accepted that some ambiguity exists when pupils are handling 2-D shapes made from plastic or wood in that, strictly speaking, these shapes are 3-D. However, it is important that they handle such shapes in order that their understanding and language develop successfully.

- In the following activities several important shape ideas are being explored:

    equivalence – exploring the 'sameness' of shapes

    transformations – exploring reflections, rotations and translations (flips, turns and slides)

    similar shapes – 'identical' except for size

    congruent shapes – identical shapes

    affinity – shapes which belong to the same 'family' (such as family of rectangles).

- When dealing with angles three notions need to be addressed: that of dynamic angle, static angle and measuring angles:

  dynamic angle – where an angle is being created by turning, that is to say some action is implied

  static angle – where an angle forms part of a shape, or has been created without turning

  measuring angles – using apparatus such as protractors and set squares.

  It is not intended to imply that these three notions of angle be approached as separate entities: they are interrelated.

- The computer has an important role to play in developing ideas of shape and space especially when working with Logo. Programs which demonstrate and explore dynamic angles are particularly useful. Some computer based activities are included in the chapter on Using and applying mathematics in this book.

 Pages 63 – 78 may be photocopied

Activities 77 – 102

The Shape and space activities are grouped as follows:

Activities **Statements**

77 – 89 Sort 2-D and 3-D shapes in different ways and give reasons for each method of sorting

90 – 97 Recognise the (reflective) symmetry in a variety of shapes in 2 and 3 dimensions

98 – 102 Understand eight points of the compass; use clockwise and anti-clockwise appropriately

NOTES FOR TEACHERS

Activities 77 – 79

Aim
▲ to sort 2-D shapes in different ways and give reasons for each method of sorting

Notes
▲ In the following three activities pupils should be encouraged to sort the shapes on each Mastersheet into sets which 'go together'. Pupils should realise that the whole page should be sorted into several sets and not just one set sorted from the rest.

▲ It is possible that some pupils may wish to include the same shape in more than one set. They may well use two colours on these shapes.

▲ It is not the intention of the activities to steer pupils to predetermined reasons for each sorting activity but to allow them to give their own reasons.

Evaluation checkpoints
▲ able to sort 2-D shapes in different ways
▲ able to give clear reasons for each method of sorting
▲ able to describe 2-D shapes accurately

Materials: *Mastersheet A35 (p.143)*
- Pupils sort the 2-D shapes into several sets.
- They should complete the 'key' at the bottom of the Mastersheet to describe the reason for each sort.
- Several Mastersheets may be completed by each student using different sorting criteria on each sheet.
- Some pupils may well only sort into two sets (such as curved and not curved) whilst others may sort into as many as four or five sets.

Materials: *Mastersheet A36 (p.144)*
- Pupils sort the set of polygons into several sets.
- They should complete the 'key' at the bottom of the Mastersheet to describe the reason for each 'sort'.
- Several Mastersheets can be completed by each student as for Activity 77.

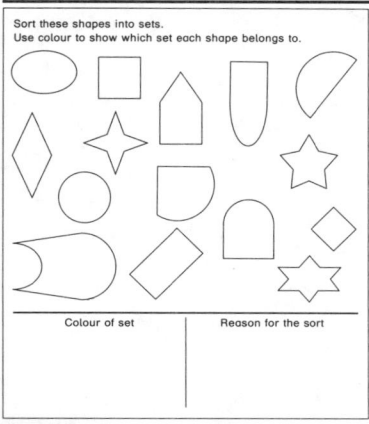

A35

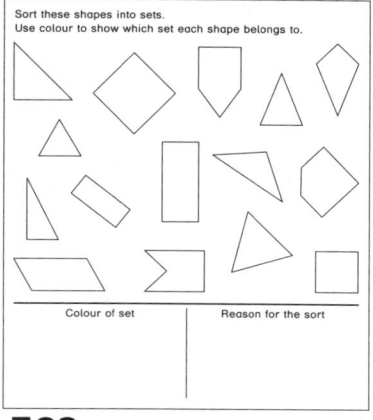

A36

MATHS BANK: Level 3   Shape and space   Page 63

NOTES FOR TEACHERS

- Pupils may be aware of the names of some of the polygons and use these terms.
- Some pupils may well sort into two sets (such as square and not square) whilst others may sort into as many as four or five sets.

Materials: *Mastersheet A37 (p.145)*

- Pupils sort the 2-D shapes into several sets.
- They should complete the 'key' at the bottom of the Mastersheet to describe the reason for each 'sort'.
- Several Mastersheets may be completed by each student as for Activity 77.
- Pupils can be encouraged to draw extra shapes on the Mastersheet which will fit into their chosen sets.

NOTES FOR TEACHERS

Activities 80 – 82

Aim
▲ to sort 3-D shapes in different ways and give reasons for each method of sorting

Notes
▲ In the following three activities pupils should be encouraged to sort the shapes on each Mastersheet into sets which 'go together'. Pupils should realise that the whole page should be sorted into several sets and not just one set sorted from the rest.

▲ It is possible that some pupils may wish to include the same shape in more than one set. They may well use two colours on these shapes.

▲ It is not the intention of the activities to steer pupils to predetermined reasons for each sorting activity but to allow them to give their own reasons.

▲ Similar activities need to be done with real objects to evaluate fully this aim.

Evaluation checkpoints
▲ can sort 3-D shapes in different ways

▲ can give clear reasons for each method of sorting

▲ can describe 3-D shapes accurately

Materials: *Mastersheet A38 (p.146)*

- Pupils sort the pictures of 3-D shapes into several sets.
- They should complete the 'key' at the bottom of the Mastersheet to describe the reason for each 'sort'.
- Several Mastersheets may be completed by each pupil using different sorting criteria on each sheet.
- Some pupils may well only sort into two sets (such as curved and not curved) whilst others may sort into as many as four or five sets.

Materials: *Mastersheet A39 (p.147)*

- Pupils sort the pictures of 'everyday' objects into several sets.
- They should complete the 'key' at the bottom of the Mastersheet to describe the reason for each sort.

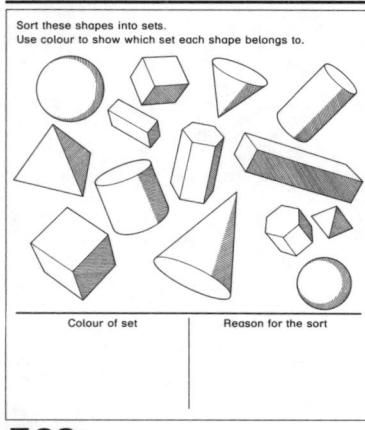

A38

A39

MATHS BANK : Level 3   Shape and space   Page 65

NOTES FOR TEACHERS

Activities 80 – 82 continued

 82 **Materials:** *Mastersheet A40 (p.148)*

- Pupils sort the diagrams of Multilink models into several sets.
- The activity can be done using Multilink shapes, if preferred. Pupils who are able to copy models from the information shown will have completed an activity appropriate to Shape and space: Level 4.
- They should complete the 'key' at the bottom of the Mastersheet to describe the reason for each 'sort'.
- They should be encouraged to try to make a new model of their own from Multilink which will fit into each of the sets.

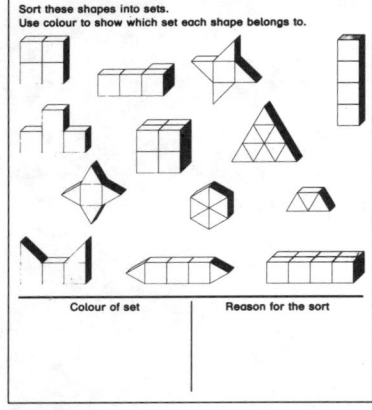

A40

NOTES FOR TEACHERS

Activities 83 – 86

Aim
▲ to sort 2-D and 3-D shapes in different ways and give reasons for each method of sorting

Notes
▲ For each of the following four activities logic blocks are sorted according to their attributes. It should be noted that although the shapes are 3-D they have 2-D names and this may need some discussion with pupils.

Evaluation checkpoints
▲ can sort 2-D and 3-D shapes in different ways
▲ can give clear reasons for each method of sorting
▲ able to use a decision tree
▲ able to use a Carroll diagram
▲ can describe shapes accurately
▲ able to use a Venn diagram

Materials: *Masersheet C4 (p.196) and logic blocks*

- Pupils sort a set of logic blocks into sets and explain the attributes of each set.
- You may wish to structure the activity such that the pupils have to sort initially into two distinct sets, then into three sets, and so on.
- Check that they can describe the attributes of each piece using shape, size, thickness, and colour.

Materials: *Masersheet A41 (p.149) and logic blocks*

- Pupils use a sorting track (decision tree) as shown on the Masersheet to sort a set of logic blocks.
- They should then be able to describe the attributes of each set of shapes collected at the ends of the track.
- A record can be kept of the sorting activity either by drawing the shapes or describing in words the shapes in the collecting area at the end of the track.

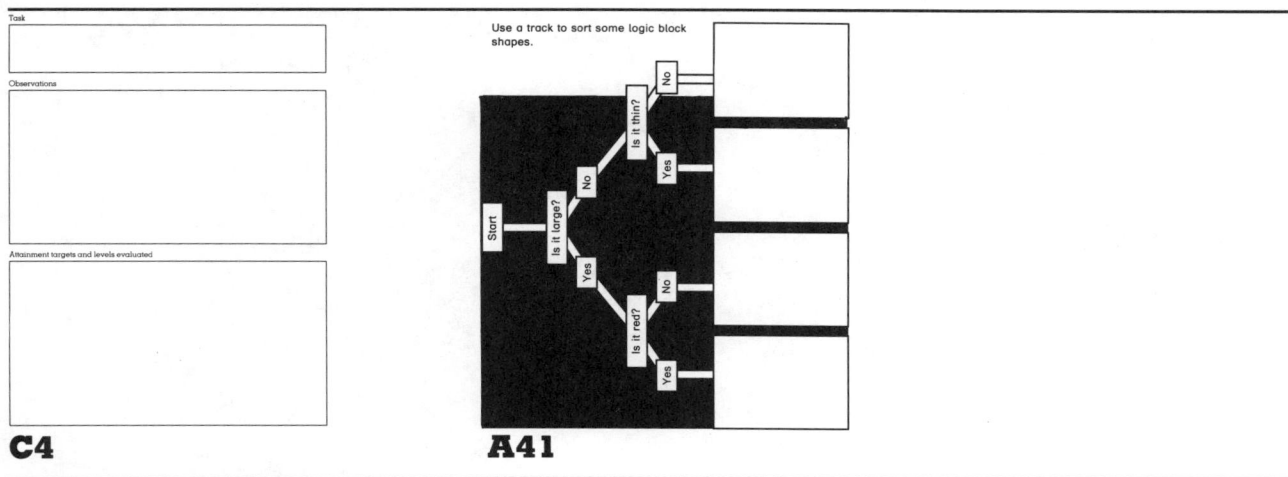

C4   A41

MATHS BANK: Level 3   Shape and space   Page 67

NOTES FOR TEACHERS

Activities 83 – 86 continued

85 **Materials:** *Mastersheet A42 (p.150) and logic blocks*

- Pupils sort a set of logic blocks onto a Carroll diagram as shown on Mastersheet A42.
- They should be able to describe the attributes of the shapes in each segment of the Carroll diagram.
- A record can be kept of the sorting activity as for Activity 84.

86 **Materials:** *Mastersheet A43 (p.151) and logic blocks*

- Pupils sort a set of logic blocks onto a Venn diagram as shown on Mastersheet A43.
- They should be able to describe the attributes of the shapes in each segment of the Venn diagram.
- A record can be kept of the sorting activity as for Activity 84.
- Note whether the children appreciate that shapes which do not go into any of the Venn circles can also be described and have attributes since the Venn diagram also includes the area outside the interlocking circles.

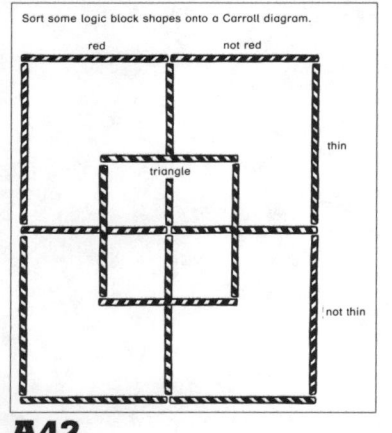

A42

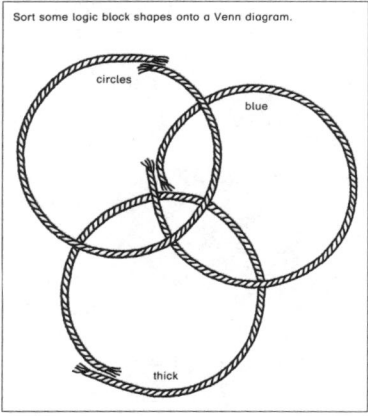

A43

Page 68 — Shape and space — MATHS BANK: Level 3

Aim

▲ to sort 2-D and 3-D shapes in different ways and give reasons for each method of sorting

Notes

▲ The following activities involve pupils in sorting 'physical' shapes, not shapes drawn on paper.

▲ Two of the activities also include using a combination of 2-D and 3-D shapes at the same time. A rich collection of plastic 2-D shapes and geometric 3-D shapes is ideal.

▲ Your observations can be entered onto Mastersheet C4 (p.196).

Evaluation checkpoints

▲ can sort 2-D and 3-D shapes in different ways

▲ can give clear reasons for each method of sorting

▲ can describe shapes accurately

Materials: a collection of 2-D and 3-D shapes

- Pupils sort the collection of shapes into sets giving reasons for their 'sort'.
- They should then be encouraged to find different reasons for sorting the same set of shapes.
- It may be necessary to reassure them that more than two sets are permitted for some 'sorts'.
- Pupils can record their sorting with the actual shapes or they can informally record their work on one of the Mastersheets C1, C2 or C3 (pp.193 – 5).

Materials: a collection of 2-D and 3-D shapes

- Pupils work in small groups.
- Turns are taken for one pupil to decide on a category of shapes s/he wants sorted from the collection but without informing the other(s). S/he then takes one or two shapes from the collection which fit the category chosen.
- The remaining pupil(s) tries to find out the classification by offering shapes from those remaining which are then either accepted or rejected.
- When all the shapes which fit the chosen category have been offered and accepted the 'chooser' must state so.
- The 'chooser' must select a category into which at least four shapes must fit. S/he must realise that the activity is not meant to be competitive.

NOTES FOR TEACHERS

Activities 87 – 89 continued

 Materials: Multilink cubes

- Pupils work in small groups.
- Teacher or pupils make a 'posting-hole' from Multilink, as shown below.

- Shapes are made using eight Multilink cubes such that they will pass through the posting-hole.
- Once such a collection of shapes has been made pupils have to re-sort the posted shapes into categories.
- When the categories have been decided a further challenge is for the children to try to make several shapes, one for each of the categories, and which still pass through the posting-hole.

Activities 90 – 93

NOTES FOR TEACHERS

Aim
▲ to recognise (reflective) symmetry in a variety of 2-D shapes

Notes
▲ The following activities will allow pupils to explore reflective symmetry in a variety of 2-D shapes, shapes which are 'geometric' as well as those which are less so.

▲ Mirrors are often used to test for reflective symmetry. However, this can cause some confusion for a few pupils. A mirror has the effect of making any shape 'become symmetrical' in that the part of the shape in front of the mirror and its reflection creates a new shape which is, of course, symmetrical.

▲ Pupils will be looking for mirror lines in various shapes as well as making shapes which are symmetrical and completing shapes to make them symmetrical.

▲ The mirror lines will not always be vertical in each case.

Evaluation checkpoints
▲ able to complete symmetrical drawings
▲ able to identify some lines of symmetry on 2-D shapes
▲ able to draw symmetrical shapes

Materials: *Mastersheet A44 (p.152)*
● Pupils complete each part picture in order to make the whole picture symmetrical.
● Although the grid lines are there to help in the drawing of the other half of each picture absolute precision is not expected.

Materials: *Mastersheet A45 (p.153)*
● Lines of symmetry should be shown on each shape where appropriate. Some shapes have no lines of symmetry whilst others will have more than one.
● Check that pupils show more than one line where appropriate.
● The shapes may be named by pupils.

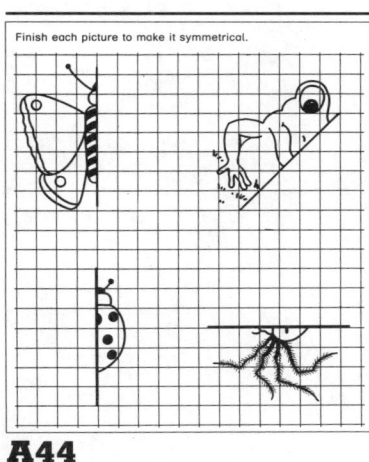
A44

A45

MATHS BANK : Level 3   Shape and space

NOTES FOR TEACHERS

Activities 90 – 93 continued

92 **Materials:** *Mastersheet A46 (p.154)*

- Pupils draw shapes onto the picture which has been started on the Mastersheet.
- Every detail in the final picture must have lines of symmetry although the whole picture itself need not be symmetrical.
- How much licence you allow for freehand drawing of symmetrical shapes is a matter for your discretion.

93 **Materials:** *Mastersheet C1, C2 or C3 (pp.193 – 5)*

- Ask pupils to write words using capital letters such that each letter has a line of symmetry.
- Challenge them to find words which only have letters with:

  vertical lines of symmetry

  horizontal lines of symmetry

  no lines of symmetry.

A46

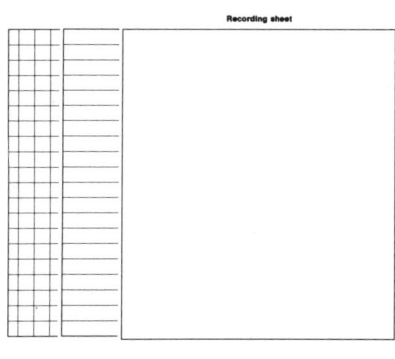

C1 C2 C3

NOTES FOR TEACHERS
Activities 94 – 97

Aim

to recognise (reflective) symmetry in a variety of shapes in 2 and 3 dimensions

Notes

▲ The following activities allow pupils to explore symmetry using real objects, developing early ideas on planes of symmetry rather than restricting them to lines of symmetry.

▲ Whether you use the term 'plane of symmetry' is a matter for your discretion, although there is no need to at this Level. Pupils need only to identify reflective symmetry in a variety of shapes.

▲ Your observations can be made on Mastersheet C4.

Evaluation checkpoints

▲ can complete symmetrical shapes

▲ can make symmetrical shapes

▲ can make symmetrical models

▲ can identify some planes of symmetry

94 **Materials:** *Mastersheet A47 (p.155), pegboard and pegs*

- Stretch an elastic band across a pegboard to halve it and act as a mirror line.
- Pupils work in pairs taking turns to make a pattern or shape with pegs on one side of the board in order that his/her partner can make the reflection of the pattern or shape.
- Observations can be made on Mastersheet C4 if pupils are not making a permanent record of any of their work. Alternatively, Mastersheet A47 can be used if a permanent record is preferred.

95 **Materials:** *Mastersheet C4*

- During PE pupils can work in pairs taking turns for one of the pair to act as the reflection of the other using slow movement.

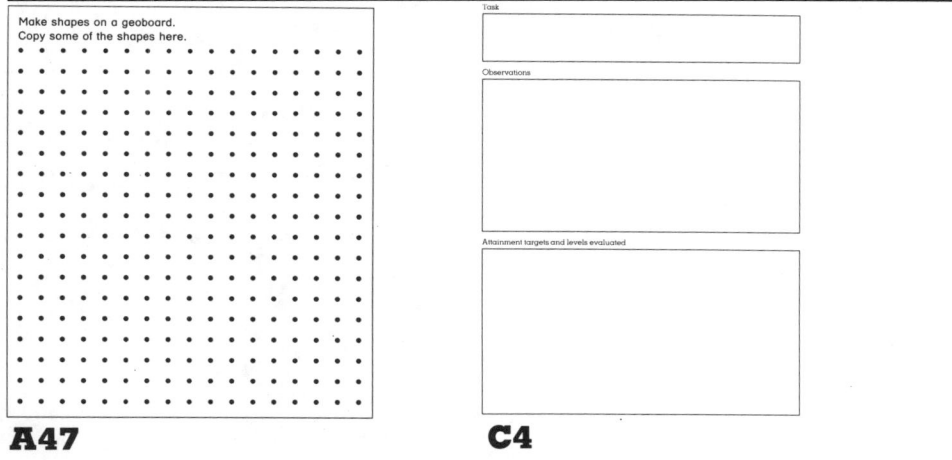

MATHS BANK: Level 3   Shape and space   Page 73

Activities 94 – 97 continued

NOTES FOR TEACHERS

Materials: *Mastersheet C4, Multilink shapes, Multilink pegboard*

- Stretch an elastic band across a Multilink pegboard in order to halve it and to act as a mirror line.

- Pupils work in pairs taking turns to make a shape or pattern with Multilink shapes in order that his/her partner can make the reflection of the pattern or shape.

- Multilink allows for models to be built 'up' from the pegboard and does not restrict pupils to two dimensions.

Materials: *Mastersheet C4 and Clixi or Polydron*

- Pupils make 3-D models from Clixi shapes (or similar 'clip-together' shapes) such that each model they make is symmetrical.

- Question them as to where each model could be chopped exactly in half, in other words, ask them to identify a plane of symmetry.

- Pupils can also make models which have no symmetry.

Task

Observations

Attainment targets and levels evaluated

C4

Notes for Teachers

Activities 98 – 100

Aim
▲ to understand eight points of the compass
▲ to use clockwise and anticlockwise appropriately

Notes
▲ Check that pupils can use a compass correctly, by lining up the marked North with the needle.
▲ Using a real compass on location helps overcome the perception that North is always vertical at the top of a page.
▲ It is worth noting that compass direction and clockwise/anticlockwise are 'impersonal', unambiguous terms whereas front, back, left, right are 'personal' terms and as such can lead to ambiguity. Pupils need to be aware of both 'personal' and 'impersonal' directions.

Evaluation checkpoints
▲ knows eight points of the compass
▲ knows clockwise and anticlockwise
▲ able to use a compass
▲ able to use 'personal' directions (such as left, right)

Materials: *Mastersheet A48 (p.156) and a compass*

- Pupils go into the playground area with a compass and a copy of Mastersheet A48.
- Each pupil's observation point can either be predetermined by you or be his/her free choice and recorded on the Mastersheet.
- They record what they can see at the eight points of the compass from their observation points.
- Discuss what they would see if they turned, for example:
  – a quarter turn anticlockwise having faced N
  – a quarter turn clockwise having faced SE

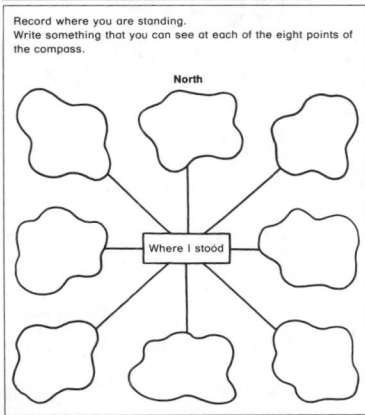
A48

Maths Bank: Level 3 Shape and space Page 75

NOTES FOR TEACHERS

Activities 98 – 100 continued

 Materials: *Mastersheet A49 (p.157)*

- Only North is marked on the compass on the Mastersheet. Pupils may add the other points if they wish.
- After answering the written questions on the Mastersheet, oral questions can be asked regarding clockwise and anticlockwise and or 'personal' directions, such as:
  - face North, turn clockwise to face South, what do you see as you turn?
  - face SE, what is directly behind you? what is to your right? what is to your left?

 Materials: *Mastersheet C4 (p.196)*

- During PE pupils can be instructed to move clockwise/anticlockwise.
- North can be marked on the hall/playground and pupils asked to move, for example, to the: NE, SW, SE, E.
- Personal directions can be used such as: left, right, front, back, side.
- Notes can be made on Mastersheet C4.

NOTES FOR TEACHERS
Activities 101 – 102

Aim
▲ to understand the notion of turning through angles less than a right-angle
▲ to understand clockwise and anticlockwise
▲ to know the eight points of the compass

Notes
▲ When considering notions of angle two important ideas occur, that of static angles and that of dynamic angles. Dynamic angles are about movement and direction such as turning clockwise/anticlockwise and bearings. Static angles are about angles which are 'fixed' such as looking at the angles which make up a triangle or quadrilateral. Measuring and drawing angles with protractors are appropriate to Measures.

▲ The following activities are concerned with angles being formed by turning. Either right-angles or fractions of right-angles can be used to describe an amount of turn or early ideas of degrees as a measurement of turn can be used.

▲ Observations about pupil understanding can be made on Mastersheet C4.

Evaluation checkpoints
▲ knows clockwise and anticlockwise
▲ knows right angles are a measure of turn
▲ can estimate parts of right-angles
▲ knows eight points of the compass
▲ can estimate multiples of right-angles

Materials: *Mastersheet B4 (p.188)*

● The two circles are cut out from Mastersheet B4 and slotted together to make an 'angle-former'.

● An angle can be seen 'growing' by turning clockwise (or anticlockwise).

● Ask pupils to use the angle-former to show:
 – a right-angle
 – half a right-angle
 – an angle more than a right-angle
 – an angle less than a right-angle.

Estimating degrees can be used if you feel it appropriate.

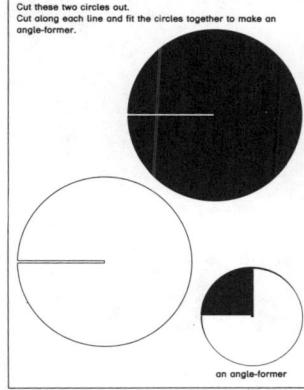

B4

MATHS BANK : Level 3   Shape and space   Page 77

NOTES FOR TEACHERS

Activities 101 – 102 continued

Materials: Use Mastersheet B5 (p.189)

- The circle and pointer are cut out from Mastersheet B5 and clipped together with a paper fastener in the centre of the circle.
- The arrow printed on the circle can be used to represent North if you wish.
- Pupils line up the pointer with the arrow and then move the pointer to show directions such as:
  - a quarter turn clockwise
  - a quarter turn anticlockwise
  - where NE is
  - where SW is
- The pointer can be moved to estimate: parts of right-angles; multiples of right-angles; degrees.

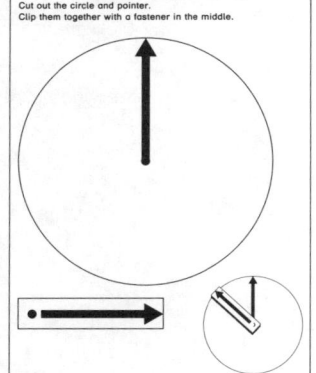

B5

Handling data

Introduction

The Handling data activities assess whether pupils are able to:

- extract pieces of information from table and lists
- enter and access information in a simple database
- construct and interpret bar charts
- create and interpret graphs (pictograms) where the symbol represents a group of units
- place events in order of 'likelihood' and use appropriate words to identify the chance
- understand and use the idea of 'evens' and say whether events are more or less likely than this
- distinguish between 'fair' and 'unfair'

The grouping of the activities is shown overleaf, while their relationship to the National Curriculum statements of attainment is shown on pages 207 – 8.

Data handling is much more than being able to represent information in graphical form using the appropriate recording skills. At best the information should be generated by the pupils themselves as the result of some investigation or 'research'. It is concerned with estimation, approximation, uncertainty as well as accuracy and definite conclusion.

When evaluating pupils' ability to record data satisfactorily, consider whether they have given thought to the order in which their information is arranged, that is to say whether or not the data is sorted after collection and before representation. Pupils often only represent data in the order in which it is collected.

The criteria for the order of bars on a bar chart are worthy of discussion. The order is sometimes predetermined by the type of data being collected (such as days of the week, months, times). On other occasions the order may be random (such as names of pupils, favourite items) and it may be sensible to draw the bars in frequency order. Pupils will also need to be familiar with bar charts which are horizontal as well as vertical.

It is also worth considering when it is appropriate to have a little space between the bars, such as when the bars have no relationship to each other (for example, names of pupils). Information such as days of the week is perhaps best represented without space between the bars as the data is 'continuous'.

Pupils need to give careful thought to the numbering of the axes, especially whether to number the lines or the spaces. Where scale is concerned the lines should be numbered so that the intermediate points can be read off. As a general rule it is better to number lines rather than spaces.

 Pages 81 – 92 may be photocopied

Activities 103 – 127

The Handling data activities are grouped as follows:

Activities **Statements**

103 – 107 extract pieces of information from table and lists

108 enter and access information in a simple database

109 – 114 construct and interpret bar charts

115 – 117 create and interpret graphs (pictograms) where the symbol represents a group of units

118 – 120 place events in order of 'likelihood' and use appropriate words to identify the chance

121 – 124 understand and use the idea of 'evens' and say whether events are more or less likely than this

125 – 127 distinguish between 'fair' and 'unfair'

Notes for Teachers

Activities 103 – 107

Aim
▲ to extract specific pieces of information from tables and lists

Notes
▲ The following five activities allow pupils to extract information from a variety of lists and tables. It is worth noting that although this statement of attainment is only concerned with extracting specific pieces of information the potential exists for you to use each table and list for other questions and activities of your choosing.

Evaluation checkpoints
▲ can extract information from lists
▲ can extract information from tables
▲ knows alphabetical order
▲ appreciates value of numerical order

Materials: *Mastersheet A50 (p.158)*
- Mastersheet A50 is an extract from a 'telephone directory'.
- It offers the potential for alphabetical ordering of lists.

Materials: *Mastersheet A51 (p.159)*
- Mastersheet A51 is an extract adapted from an intercity train timetable.
- It offers the opportunity to discuss the 24 hour clock.
- Using timetables to estimate times of arrival is appropriate to Handling data: Level 4.

Materials: *Mastersheet A52 (p.160)*
- Mastersheet A52 is a simple price list.

Materials: *Mastersheet A53 (p.161)*
- Mastersheet A53 shows Division 1 League Football Table as at January 1 1991.

Materials: *Mastersheet A54 (p.162)*
- Mastersheet A54 is the multiplication tables up to 10x10.

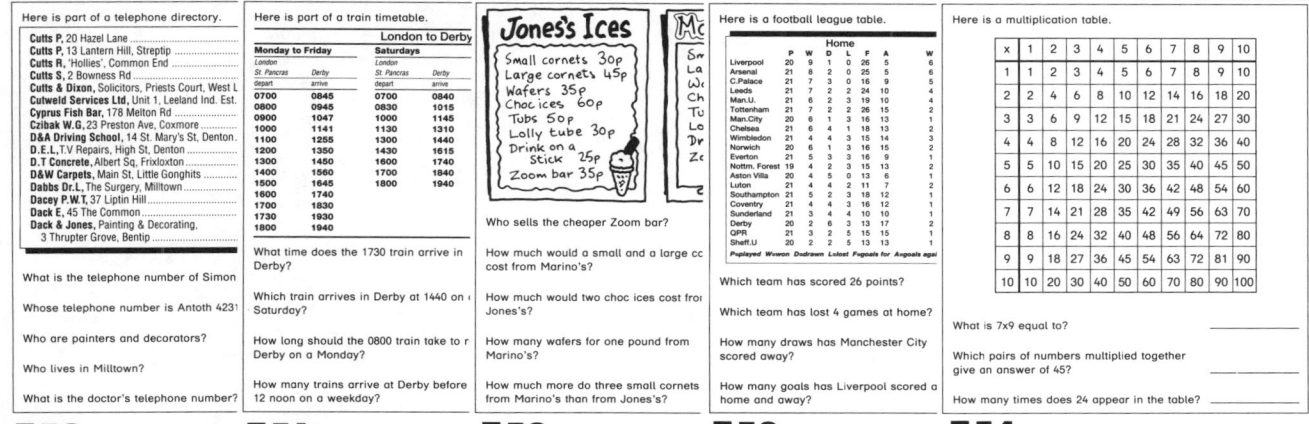

A50   **A51**   **A52**   **A53**   **A54**

Maths Bank: Level 3   Handling data   Page 81

NOTES FOR TEACHERS — Activity 108

Aim
▲ to enter and access information in a simple database

Notes
▲ Because of the range of computers and variety of software available for each machine it is difficult to suggest program specific activities to evaluate this particular statement of attainment. Another difficulty is the increasingly widespread use of locally based datafiles and LEA specific software. Much database work stems from integrated topic work and is not appropriate for the format of this book.

▲ Some commercial and local databases have information already on file for pupils to access, for example files on birds and on local census figures.

▲ When pupils are accessing information it may be worth noting if they can use one or more fields for the search.

▲ Some databases will print out a variety of graphs to show information on file. Pupils need to be made aware that nonsensical graphs which have no relevance can often be printed out. Caution needs to be exercised over abuse of the graphical facilities in programs.

▲ Sorting collected information according to various criteria is an important aspect of data handling. Programs which have pre-determined sorting criteria built into them need treating with care because they reduce pupil contribution in the actual sorting process.

▲ It is worth noting that the ability to interrogate a computer database is appropriate to Handling data: Level 4.

Evaluation checkpoints
▲ able to enter facts into a database
▲ able to access information in a database
▲ able to search using one field
▲ able to search on more than one field
▲ able to use graphic facilities sensibly
▲ able to edit a database

Materials: *Mastersheet C6 (p.198)*

● Mastersheet C6 is appropriate for you to make observations on pupils using a database.

Name of Database Program

Title of topic

Entering data

Accessing data

General comments

C6

NOTES FOR TEACHERS

Activities 109 – 111

Aim
▲ to construct and interpret bar charts

Notes
▲ Several important aspects of drawing bar charts need to be evaluated:
 – selecting an appropriate scale
 – correct labelling and numbering of axes
 – deciding whether to draw the bars horizontally or vertically
 – deciding whether there can be space between the bars
 – deciding whether the order of the bars is random or 'fixed'
 – deciding whether to sort the data before graphing

▲ An aspect that is often overlooked is that of deciding whether the order of the bars can be changed (such as the names of pupils) or whether they are 'fixed' (such as days of the week). If the order is random then perhaps sorting the data into an order before representing it on a graph might be appropriate.

▲ There is a space on each Mastersheet for pupils to graph the data. Mastersheet C1 can also be used, if required.

▲ The data for graphing is provided in the activities below. The generation of own data by pupils can be found in the chapter on Using and Applying Mathematics (pp.93 – 108).

Evaluation checkpoints
▲ can choose appropriate scales
▲ can label sensibly
▲ knows when to sort before drawing
▲ can use horizontal and vertical bars
▲ can interpret bar charts

Materials: *Mastersheet A55 (p.163)*

● Mastersheet A55 shows data of days of the week upon which some birthdays fall.

● The order of the bars is 'fixed'.

● It would be inappropriate for there to be space between the bars.

Several people were asked on which day of the week their birthdays were held.
Draw a graph to show the information.

Days	Sun	Mon	Tue	Wed	Thu	Fri	Sat
Number of people	16	7	23	15	20	8	19

Write two things you can find out from your graph:

A55

MATHS BANK: Level 3   Handling data   Page 83

NOTES FOR TEACHERS

Activities 109 – 111 continued

 110 **Materials:** *Mastersheet A56 (p.164)*

- Mastersheet A56 shows a tally of a traffic survey.
- The order of the bars can be 'random', allowing for the bars to be arranged in order of frequency.
- There can be space between the bars and they can be drawn vertically or horizontally.
- Pupils may need to be reassured that there is a range of possible vehicles which could go under the heading of 'other' (such as tricycles, horses, pick-up trucks).

 111 **Materials:** *Mastersheet A57 (p.165)*

- Mastersheet A57 records favourite flavours of crisps.
- The order of the bars can be 'random', allowing for the bars to be arranged in order of frequency.
- There can be space between the bars and they can be drawn vertically or horizontally.

NOTES FOR TEACHERS

Activities 112 – 114

Aim
▲ to interpret bar charts

Notes
▲ The following activities allow pupils to interpret a range of bar charts.

Evaluation checkpoints:
▲ able to read off horizontal axes
▲ able to read off vertical axes
▲ able to interpret the scale
▲ able to interpret vertical bar charts
▲ able to interpret horizontal bar charts

Materials: *Mastersheet A58 (p.166)*

- The bar chart on Mastersheet A58 shows days of the week against books borrowed from a village library.
- The bars are 'fixed' and it would be inappropriate to have gaps between them, because the days flow naturally from one to the next.

Materials: *Mastersheet A59 (p.167)*

- The bar chart on Mastersheet A59 shows the circumference of some tins.
- The data is 'random' so the bars have been drawn horizontally in order of circumference size.
- There can be a gap between the bars in this type of graph.

Materials: *Mastersheet A60 (p.168)*

- Mastersheet A60 shows the number of children with birthdays in each month.
- The bars are 'fixed' and it would be inappropriate to have gaps between them, because the months flow naturally from one to the next.

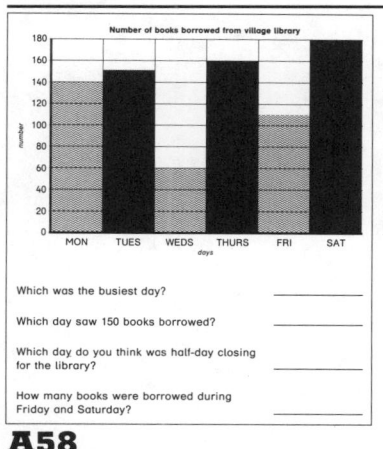

A58

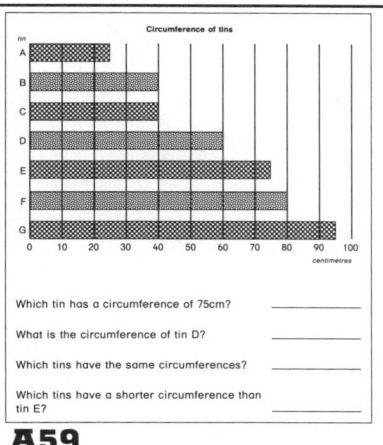

A59

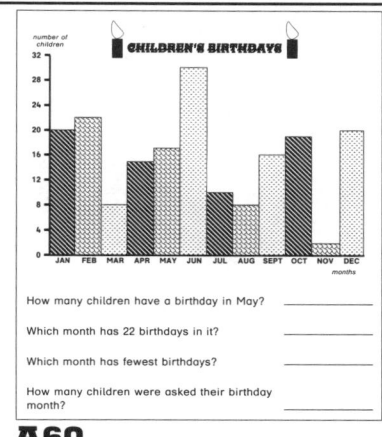

A60

MATHS BANK : Level 3   Handling data   Page 85

NOTES FOR TEACHERS

Activities 115 – 117

Aim
▲ to create and interpret graphs (pictograms) where the symbol represents a group of units

Notes
▲ The data for graphing is provided in the three activities below. The generation of own data by pupils can be found in the chapter on Using and applying mathematics.

▲ There is a space on Mastersheets A62 and A63 for pupils to graph the data; otherwise, Mastersheets C1, C2 or C3 can be used.

▲ Unlike bar charts where the reading between two numbers on the axis can be read accurately, the value of a 'part' symbol in pictograms may only be 'an estimate' especially when scale is involved. Pupils will have to decide when to use a 'part symbol' and when, or whether, to round up or down and use a whole symbol.

Evaluation checkpoints
▲ can draw sensible pictograms
▲ can use scale
▲ can estimate when using 'part symbols'
▲ labels pictograms correctly
▲ provides a key for the symbol
▲ can interpret a pictogram

Materials: *Mastersheet A61 (p.169)*

● Mastersheet A61 shows two pictograms for pupils to consider.

● The scale is different on each pictogram and pupils should appreciate the approximate nature of the large numbers involved.

Materials: *Mastersheet A62 (p.170)*

● Mastersheet A62 shows data concerned with numbers of people visiting a cinema complex.

● Check that pupils:
 – select a sensible scale for their pictogram symbol
 – round up or down and use part symbols sensibly
 – provide a key to show what their symbol stands for
 – label the pictogram appropriately

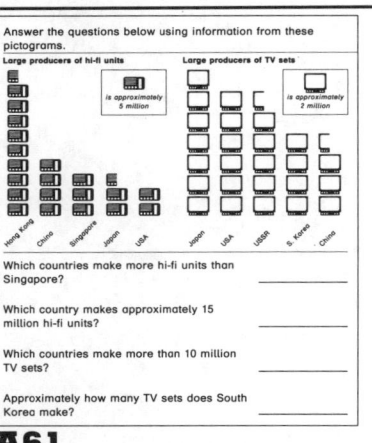

A61

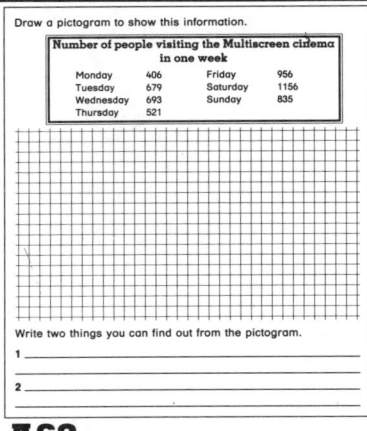

A62

Page 86   Handling data   MATHS BANK: Level 3

NOTES FOR TEACHERS — Activities 115 – 117 continued

117 Materials: *Mastersheet A63 (p.171)*

- Mastersheet A63 shows data on the crisp eating habits of several classes of children.
- Check that pupils:
  - select a sensible scale for their pictogram symbol
  - round up or down and use part symbols sensibly
  - provide a key to show what their symbol stands for
  - label the pictogram appropriately

Draw a pictogram to show this information.

Bags of crisps eaten by each class during one week

Class 1	102	Class 4	115
Class 2	63	Class 5	89
Class 3	153	Class 6	94

Write two things you can find out from the pictogram.

1. _____
2. _____

A63

NOTES FOR TEACHERS

Activities 118 – 120

Aim
▲ to place events in the order of 'likelihood'
▲ to use appropriate words to identify the chance

Notes
▲ It is not necessary to use formal 'statistical' language such as 'probability'; everyday terms used to describe chance (such as likely, possible, doubtful) are quite satisfactory.

Evaluation checkpoints
▲ can place events in order of 'likelihood'
▲ can use appropriate words to describe the 'chance'

Materials: *Mastersheet A64 (p.172)*
- Mastersheet A64 depict happenings which may or may not occur. Each pupil's responses may well differ depending upon his/her individual circumstances.
- More than one picture may well be joined to the same 'chance' outcome.
- Pupils should be able to justify their responses and use appropriate language such as 'no chance,' 'maybe'.

Materials: *Mastersheet A65 (p.173)*
- Pupils list some events which they consider certain, possible, doubtful and impossible in the spaces provided on the Mastersheet.
- The criteria for the events can be a free choice on the part of pupils or within a context set by you such as:
  - things which will happen today
  - things 'I can do'.

Materials: *Mastersheet A66 (p.174)*
- Students should realise that they may use several words to describe each event.
- If several words are used to match each event check that they more or less mean the same 'chance' (such as: definitely, positive, sure, no doubt ...)

A64

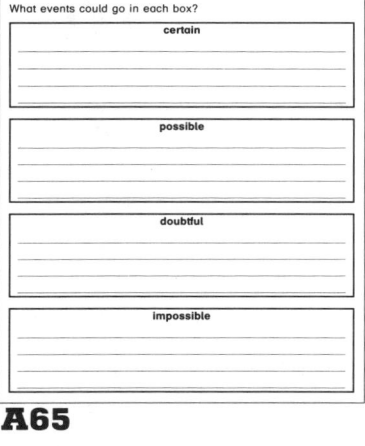

A65

A66

NOTES FOR TEACHERS

Activities 121 – 124

Aim
▲ to understand and use the idea of 'evens'
▲ to say whether events are more or less likely than 'evens'

Notes
▲ Pupils should realise that, when experimenting to find out about 'evens', a certain amount of approximation is called for. For example, tossing a coin to check on the likelihood of obtaining heads or tails is unlikely to produce exactly the same number of heads and tails over a small number of trials. At Level 3 it might be appropriate to accept language such as 'about the same chance'.

▲ A particular problem with experimenting to discover the likelihood of an event happening is the 'large' number of trials necessary to produce acceptable results. Boredom can quickly result if one pupil has to conduct all the trials entirely on his/her own. It might be appropriate for a group of pupils to each conduct some of the trials and then to combine their results.

▲ Below are some suggested activities for pupils to decide whether the chance of an event happening is even, more than even or less than even. How many and which you choose to use is a matter for your discretion. Pupils can record the estimation and result of each experiment on copies of Mastersheet A67: if extra recording space is needed then use Mastersheet C1, C2 or C3.

Evaluation checkpoints
▲ understands the idea of 'evens'
▲ can state whether events are more or less likely than 'evens'

Materials: *Mastersheet A67 (p.175) and Mastersheet B6 (p.190)*
● Mastersheet B6, shows a variety of spinners which can be photocopied onto thin card and used with a cocktail stick. Alternatively, standard dice can be adapted by sticking paper on the faces.
● For selected spinners/dice ask pupils: *'What is the chance of obtaining, (for example): an odd number? a black spot? a four?'*

Materials: *Mastersheet A67 and playing cards*
● Ask pupils: *'What is the chance of turning up a, (for example): red card? picture card? diamond? card worth more than 3?'*

A67   **B6**

MATHS BANK : Level 3   Handling data   Page 89

NOTES FOR TEACHERS

Activities 121 – 124 continued

Materials: *Mastersheet A67 and dominoes*
- Ask pupils: *'What is the chance of turning over (for example): a double six? an even total? a total of more than five?'*

Materials: *Mastersheet A67 and Multilink cubes*
- Place an equal number of red and yellow cubes in a bag.
- On Mastersheet A67 pupils record the chance of drawing out a red cube.
- Several trials are undertaken to check what happens.
- More red cubes than yellow cubes are placed in a bag and the activity is repeated.
- Repeat with fewer red cubes than yellow cubes in the bag.

NOTES FOR TEACHERS

Activities 125 – 127

Aim
▲ to distinguish between 'fair' and 'unfair'

Notes
▲ For each of the activities below pupils enter their 'predictions' and comments on Mastersheet C7.

▲ It is a common misconception for pupils to think that if s/he 'loses' a game then it must have been 'unfair'! Pupils should be encouraged to give a reason why they consider an activity to be 'fair'/'unfair'.

Evaluation checkpoints
▲ can distinguish between 'fair' and 'unfair'
▲ can make up 'fair' and 'unfair' rules

Materials: *Mastersheet B6 (p.190), Mastersheet C7 (p.199) and Multilink cubes*

- Pupils work in pairs sharing spinners D, E and F cut out from Mastersheet B6 (or use adapted dice similarly marked).
- One pupil collects white Multilink cubes and the other black cubes as designated by the white or black spots on the spinners.
- Turns are taken to twist spinner A and collect a cube if it lands on her/his colour spot. First to collect ten cubes of her/his colour wins the game.
- Students have to decide if this is a 'fair' game and enter their ideas on Mastersheet C7, then play the game to find out what happens.
- Will the fairness of the game be altered if spinner E or F is used instead of spinner D?

Materials: *Mastersheet B2 (p.186) and Mastersheet C7*

- Pupils work in pairs, one having the digits 0, 2, 4, 6, 8 and the other 1, 3, 5, 7, 9 cut from Mastersheet B2. (Note: it is not intended to imply that the digit 0 is even.)
- Each pupil puts his/her digits into sets, each set comprising two or more digits.
- A point is scored for each set which has an odd total. Is this a 'fair' game?
- Would it be a 'fair' game if points were scored for even totals?

B6

C7

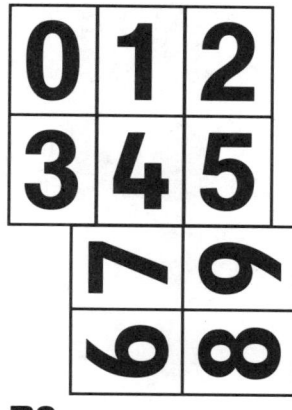

B2

MATHS BANK : Level 3   Handling data   Page 91

NOTES FOR TEACHERS

Activities 125 – 127 continued

127

Materials: *Mastersheet C7 and a pack of playing cards*

- Pupils work in pairs with a shuffled pack of playing cards between them, face down.
- The picture cards have values as follows: Jack = 11, Queen = 12, King = 13.
- One pupil is the 'odds/evens' player, the other the 'red/black' player.
- The odds/evens player starts by guessing whether the top card, when turned over, will be odd (or even). If the guess is correct the player keeps the card, if incorrect the card goes on a discard pile.
- In a similar way the red/black player guesses if the new top card, when turned over, will be red (or black), keeps it if correct or discards it if incorrect.
- Turns are taken until the pack is exhausted. The winner is the player with most cards at the end of the game.
- Pupils should discuss whether this is a 'fair' or 'unfair' game.
- Challenge them to find a 'fair' guessing rule for each player and an 'unfair' rule.

C7

Handling data MATHS BANK: Level 3

Using and applying mathematics

Introduction

The activities in the Using and applying mathematics section assess whether children are able to:

- select the materials and the mathematics to use for a task; check results and consider whether they are sensible.
- explain work being done and record findings systematically
- make and test predictions

During the course of these activities it is worth bearing the following points in mind:

- Some may be lengthy pieces of work, others may be much shorter. The lengthy problems and investigations need not be attempted and completed at one 'sitting'. It may sometimes be advisable for pupils to work at them in shorter blocks of time over a longer period.
- The activities should be integrated into normal classroom work.
- They also offer opportunities for evaluation in other areas of the curriculum, such as English, Science, Craft and Design Technology.
- Most of the activities allow for pupils to be evaluated independently whilst they are working as the member of a small group.
- Each activity allows pupils to operate at various levels of sophistication so enabling everyone to gain success. That is to say the activities are not 'Level 3 activities' but ones which allow you to evaluate whether Level 3 statement of attainments are being satisfied.

The activities include problems which use the environment, 'real' problems and mathematical problems. Pupils need experience of all these types.

Your observations can be made on Mastersheet C4 and pupils can record on Mastersheets C1, C2 or C3 as appropriate.

Of the procedures adopted by pupils, some worthy of evaluation at Level 3 include those listed below:

- explores the problem and is willing to make trials and guesses at the start of the exercise
- collects information, records, sorts and orders and represents it sensibly
- uses a systematic approach
- checks results and knows whether they are sensible
- uses little needless repetition
- looks for and recognises simple patterns
- uses one solution to find others

- uses trial and improvement techniques
- uses sensible apparatus and materials to 'solve' the problem
- communicates about the problem clearly
- makes and tests simple predictions

 Pages 95 – 108 may be photocopied

Activities 128 – 147

The activities in the Using and applying mathematics section are grouped as follows:

Activities Statements

128 – 147
- select the materials and the mathematics to use for a task;
- check results and consider whether they are sensible;
- explain work being done and record findings systematically
- make and test predictions

NOTES FOR TEACHERS

Activities 128 – 129

Aim
- ▲ to select the materials and the mathematics to use for a task
- ▲ to check results and consider whether they are sensible
- ▲ to explain work being done and record findings systematically
- ▲ make and test predictions

Notes
- ▲ Unlike the other activities in this book no attempt has been made to focus on the separate statements of attainments.
- ▲ Suggestions for evaluations have been listed in the Introduction to this chapter on page 93.
- ▲ Your comments can be shown on the pupil Mastersheet where appropriate and/or on observation Mastersheet C4.

128 **Materials:** *Mastersheet A68 (p.176)*

- Pupils should realise that the number written on each truck is the total of its two wheels.
- When finding solutions to problem 'A' on the Mastersheet they should realise that there is more than one solution and attempt to find them all.
- There is no solution (using positive numbers) for problem 'B'. Pupils should be encouraged to try to explain in a simple way why this is so.
- Results can be shown on Mastersheet A68 or on Mastersheet C1, C2 or C3.
- You can open up this simple little investigation by giving pupils a picture of an empty truck like this one:

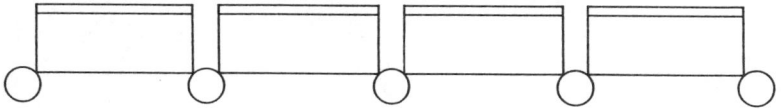

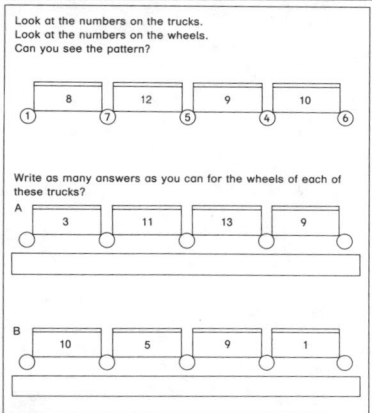

A68

Maths Bank: Level 3 Using and applying mathematics Page 95

NOTES FOR TEACHERS

Activities 128 – 129 continued

Pupils can be challenged to write numbers on the trucks such that using positive numbers:

- there are several possible solutions
- there are no possible solutions
- there is only one solution
- there are more than four solutions

129

Materials: *Mastersheet C1, C2 or C3 and a thermometer*

- Pupils find the temperature of some cold water.
- They then find the temperature of some 'warm' water.
- Challenge them to make a mixture which has a temperature arbitrarily chosen by you which lies between these two.
- Discussion may centre around issues such as: *'Does the amount of water need to be the same for each testing? Has the thermometer to be in the water for the same length of time for each trial? Does the thermometer have to return to 'normal' after each testing?'*

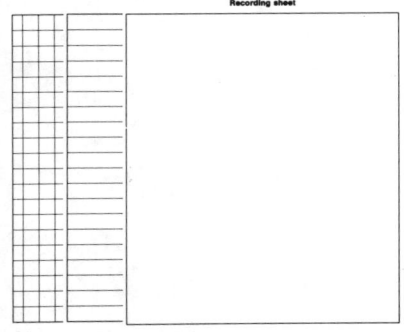

C1 C2 C3

Page 96   Using and applying mathematics   **Maths Bank: Level 3**

NOTES FOR TEACHERS

Activities 130 – 131

Aim
▲ to select the materials and the mathematics to use for a task
▲ to check results and consider whether they are sensible
▲ to explain work being done and record findings systematically
▲ make and test predictions

130
Materials: *Mastersheet A69 (p.177)*

- Pupils should record some of the 'environmental numbers' they see in their neighbourhood, such as telephone numbers, house numbers, telegraph pole numbers, bus numbers, room numbers.

- They should be encouraged to note different types of numbers and to keep only one sample of each type (for example, only one house number in the street need be recorded).

- They will need to consider how they are to present this information.

- Some simple researching may be necessary for them to discover what the numbers mean and how they are used (for example, where number 84 bus starts and ends).

131
Materials: *coffee jar lids and Plasticine*

- Pupils can make simple 'tocker' timers from a coffee jar lid into which has been placed a small roll of Plasticine.

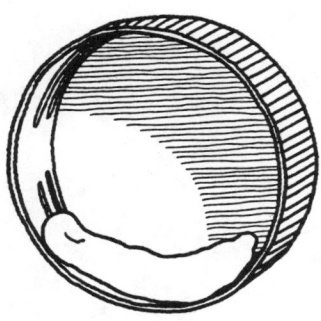
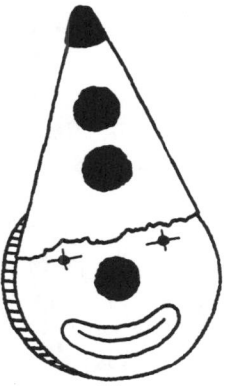

'tocker' timer

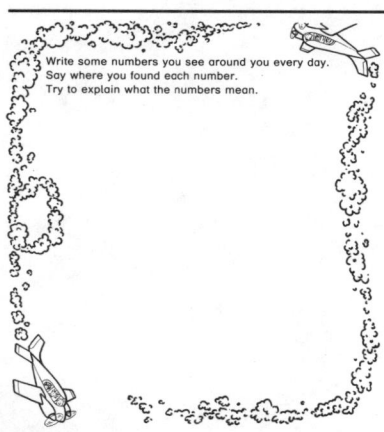

A69

MATHS BANK: Level 3   Using and applying mathematics   Page 97

NOTES FOR TEACHERS
Activities 130 – 131 continued

- A 'picture' can be fastened to one side as shown in the illustration on p.97.
- Pupils can be challenged to make a timer which satisfies certain criteria such as:
    - 'tocks' for 30 seconds
    - 'tocks' for as long as it takes to write a name and address
    - 'tocks' for as long as it takes to get ready for PE.
- Questions can be posed such as:
    - *Does the size of coffee lid affect the timing?*
    - *Does the weight of Plasticine make a difference?*
    - *Does the length of Plasticine 'roll' affect the timing?*

    A stop watch can be used in conjunction with these experiments.
- A small group of pupils can each make a 'tocker' timer then arrange them in order. Pupils should be encouraged to discuss why there is a difference in the timing of each one.
- Pupils can record their work on Mastersheet C1, C2 or C3 and your observations can be made on Mastersheet C4.

NOTES FOR TEACHERS

Activities 132 – 133

Aim

▲ to select the materials and the mathematics to use for a task

▲ to check results and consider whether they are sensible

▲ to explain work being done and record findings systematically

▲ make and test predictions

Materials: *Mastersheet B7 (p.191) and A70 (p.178)*

- Pupils cut out the two sets of numerals 0–20 from Mastersheet B7.
- They choose any set of four numerals and place them in two rows on a grid on Mastersheet A70.
- The two rows are totalled to find the 'row totals', as shown in the example below:

This arrangement of 5, 6, 9 and 12 makes 'row' totals of 14 and 18.

- Pupils try to find all the different 'row totals' which are possible (depending on the numerals selected there will be either five or six possibilities).
- The pupils then change the four numerals and repeat the activity.
- Check whether they appreciate that the reversal of the order of two numerals does not alter the 'row total' (i.e. commutative property of addition).

B7   A70

MATHS BANK: Level 3   Using and applying mathematics   Page 99

NOTES FOR TEACHERS

Activities 132 – 133 continued

- Check whether they tackle the problem in a systematic manner.
- Some pupils may be able to hypothesise why some choices only result in five possible totals; that is to say when one pair of numerals has the same total as the other (for example, 5, 9 and 10, 4).
- 'Column totals' can be explored in the same way.
- Results can be shown on Mastersheet A70.

Materials: *Mastersheets B7 and A71 (p.179)*

- Pupils cut out the two sets of numerals 0 – 20 from Mastersheet B7.
- The numerals are used to help pupils find solutions to the addition grids on Mastersheet A71. The 'row totals' and 'column totals' are shown on grids A – C.
- For each of the grids A and B there are several possible solutions. Check that pupils attempt to find them all. (The number of solutions is related to the smallest row or column total.)
- For grid C there is no solution possible. Check whether pupils can put forward some explanation as to why this cannot be done. (The sum of the 'row totals' is not the same as the sum of the 'column totals'.)
- Grid D has no totals given. This is for pupils to create their own problem which can or cannot be done. They may even be able to hypothesise as to the number of solutions their 'D' grids will have.

NOTES FOR TEACHERS

Activities 134 – 137

Aim
▲ to select the materials and the mathematics to use for a task
▲ to check results and consider whether they are sensible
▲ to explain work being done and record findings systematically
▲ make and test predictions

Materials: *Mastersheet A72 (p.180) and Multilink cubes*

- Pupils predict how many cubes it will take to make each model shown on Mastersheet A72; they then check their prediction.
- For some of the models there could be more than one acceptable answer, it is up to each pupil to justify his/her checked prediction.

Materials: *Mastersheet C1, C2 or C3 and Mastersheet C4*

- Pupils investigate the following problem:

  'Are all size 2 shoes the same length and width?'

- Obviously the size of shoe can be changed to be appropriate to the pupils undertaking this problem.
- They could be encouraged to look at the relationship between shoe sizes and length.
- Pupils can record on Mastersheet C1, C2 or C3, while you may make observations on Mastersheet C4.

Materials: *Mastersheet A73 (p.181)*

- The pupil has to make up a 'mystery trail' from a position inside the classroom to somewhere within the confines of the school or its grounds.
- S/he must decide what will be useful in helping with this task, such as compass and trundle wheel, although non-standard units such as strides and turning 'right' and 'left' may be used.
- The aims of this activity are for pupils to decide how to describe direction and distance accurately, and to choose appropriate materials and mathematics to solve a problem.

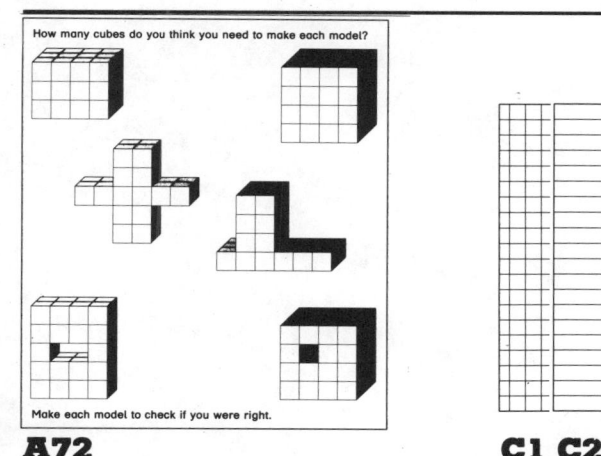

A72

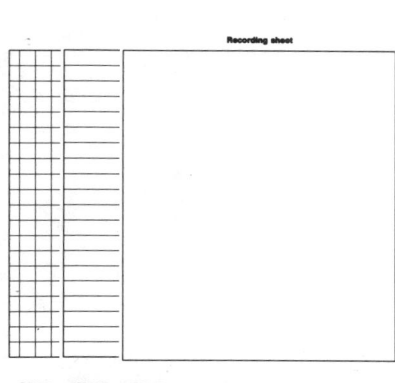

C1 C2 C3

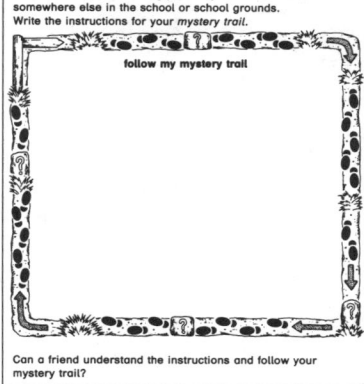

A73

MATHS BANK : Level 3   Using and applying mathematics   Page 101

NOTES FOR TEACHERS

Activities 134 – 137 continued

137 **Materials:** *Mastersheet C1, C2 or C3 and Mastersheet C4*

- Four differently shaped containers are needed, three containing an identical amount of water and the fourth containing a different amount.
- The problem is similar to the game 'find the lady' in that the pupil has to find which container has the 'odd' amount of water in it.
- Challenge the students to find the simplest test to find the 'odd one out'.
- The activity can be repeated with four identical, lidded containers, three having the same weight of sand in them, the fourth having a different weight.
- Results may be recorded as for Activity 135.

C1 C2 C3 C4

NOTES FOR TEACHERS

Activities 138 – 139

Aim
▲ to select the materials and the mathematics to use for a task
▲ to check results and consider whether they are sensible
▲ to explain work being done and record findings systematically
▲ make and test predictions

138 **Materials:** *Mastersheet C1, C2 or C3*

- Pupils make a 'display' to show where each member of the class/group is going, (or would like to go), on holiday.
- They may need reassurance that they can present the information in whatever form they wish such as: maps, lists, tables, charts.
- You may wish to stipulate the minimum information required on each display, such as: distance, approximate cost, dates, method of travel.
- Check that they can extract information from their representation.
- The representation adopted by individual pupils can be compared and contrasted by a group of pupils to discover the information which can be extracted from each.

C1 C2 C3

NOTES FOR TEACHERS

Activities 138 – 139 continued

139 **Materials:** *Mastersheet C1, C2 or C3 and Multilink Isos*

- Pupils link together eight Multilink Isos pieces to make a 'ring'.
- The Isos ring can be flexed and the shape of the hole made by the ring investigated.
- Pupils experiment with making and recording the differently shaped holes.
- The holes can be sorted and categorised.
- Pupils may notice that the perimeter of each hole shape is always eight units.
- The number of Isos in the ring can be varied.

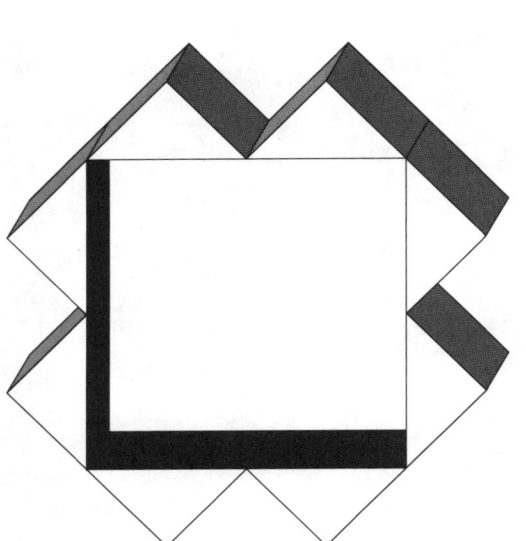 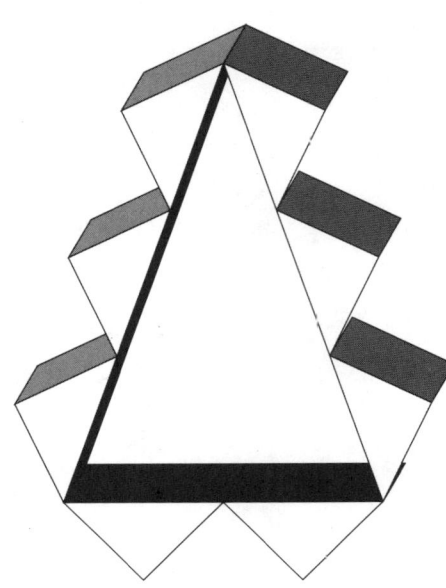

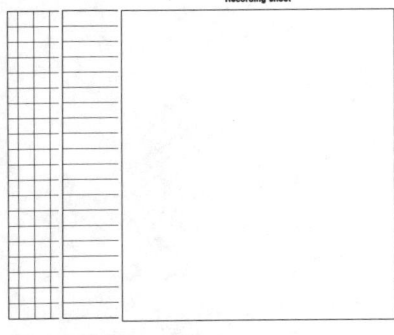

C1 C2 C3

Page 104   Using and applying mathematics   **MATHS BANK : Level 3**

NOTES FOR TEACHERS

Activities 140 – 142

Aim
- ▲ to select the materials and the mathematics to use for a task
- ▲ to check results and consider whether they are sensible
- ▲ to explain work being done and record findings systematically
- ▲ make and test predictions

Materials: *Mastersheet A74 (p.182) and logic blocks*

- Pupils place logic block shapes on Mastersheet A74 in such a way that if the 'diamonds' are joined by:
  - one line: the shapes have only one different attribute
  - two lines: the shapes have two different attributes
  - three lines: the shapes have three different attributes
- Alternative solutions can be explored.
- Check that pupils can explain their reasoning.

Materials: *Mastersheet A75 (p.183) and logic blocks*

- Pupils place logic block shapes in such a way that if the 'circles' are joined by:
  - one line: the shapes have only one different attribute
  - two lines: the shapes have two different attributes
  - three lines: the shapes have three different attributes
- Alternative solutions can be explored.
- Check that pupils can explain their reasoning.

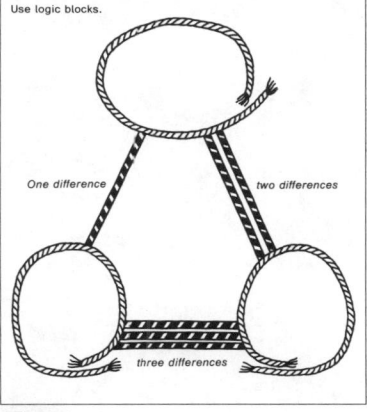

A74

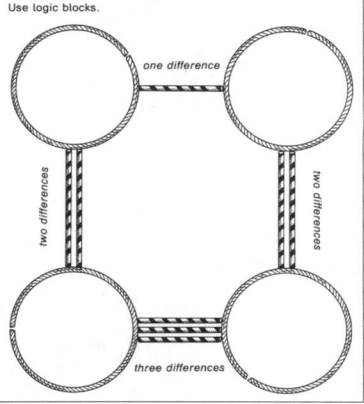

A75

MATHS BANK : Level 3 Using and applying mathematics Page 105

NOTES FOR TEACHERS

Activities 140 – 142 continued

142

Materials: *Mastersheets B8 (p.192) and C8 (p.200)*

- Pupils cut out the large triangle on Mastersheet B8 and score and fold along the black lines 'both ways' alternatively (i.e. mountain and valley folds).
- The large triangle can then be folded to make a rich variety of shapes.
- A copy of some of the shapes made can be kept on Mastersheet C8, such as by colouring them in.
- The shapes made can be sorted and classified according to a whole range of criteria, such as:
  - 4-sided shapes, 5-sided shapes
  - number of small triangles in each shape
  - symmetry
  - angles.

  Pupils should choose their own criteria for the 'sort'.
- Some of the polygons made in this way can be named.
- This activity allows pupils to explore shapes other than the set of plastic 'regular' and 'semi-regular' shapes normally available in the classroom.

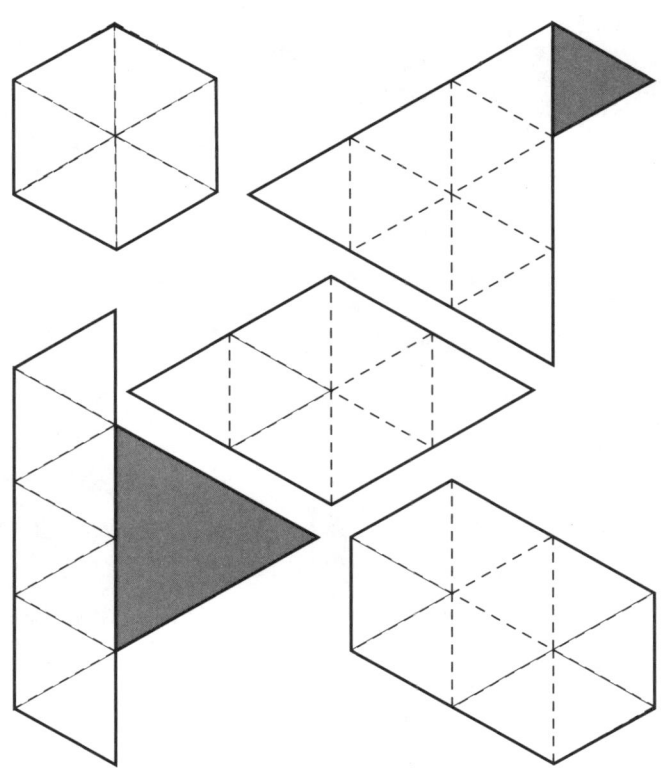

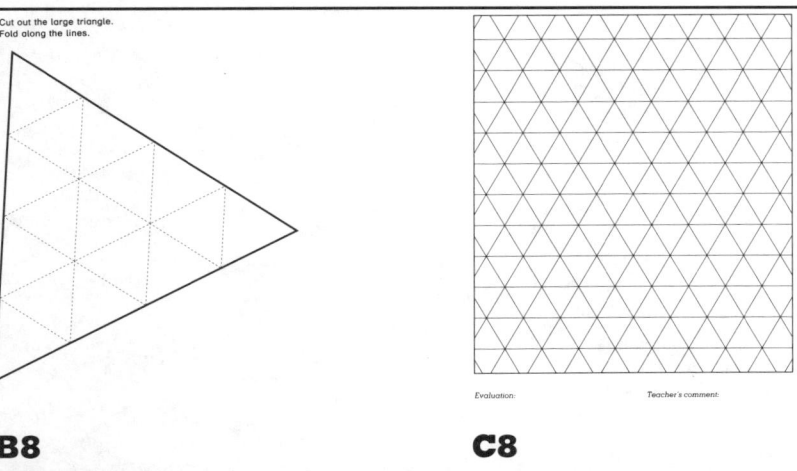

B8 **C8**

Page 106   Using and applying mathematics   **MATHS BANK**: Level 3

NOTES FOR TEACHERS

Activities 143 – 147

Aim
▲ to select the materials and the mathematics to use for a task
▲ to check results and consider whether they are sensible
▲ to explain work being done and record findings systematically
▲ make and test predictions

Materials: *Mastersheet C8 (p.200) and Clixi (or other interlocking shapes)*
- Pupils explore different '2-D shapes' which can be made from clipping together a nominated number of triangular pieces of Clixi.
- A record can be kept on Mastersheet C8 when the shapes can be sorted according to criteria selected by the pupil.
- Similarly, square Clixi or a combination of square and triangular shapes can be used.

Materials: *Mastersheet C1 (p.193), and Clixi (or other interlocking shapes)*
- Pupils can clip together square Clixi to discover which arrangements will fold up to make a cube.
- A record can be kept by copying the appropriate nets onto Mastersheet C1.

Materials: *Clixi (or other interlocking shapes)*
- Pupils have to make a 'container' from the Clixi shapes which will hold an object (or collection of objects) decided by you.

Materials: *Multilink or other interlocking cubes*
- Pupils start with 24 cubes and explore the different cuboids which can be made, each being made from all 24 cubes.
- They have to decide upon an appropriate way to keep a record of their findings.
- The number of cubes used to start with can be varied.

C8   **C1**

MATHS BANK: Level 3   Using and applying mathematics   Page 107

NOTES FOR TEACHERS

Activities 143 – 147 continued

147
- Set pupils the challenge of making up a game which uses three dimensions.
- The rules of the game must be 'fair'.
- The game could be based on a 3-D model built by the pupils such as:
  - helter skelter
  - multi storey hotel
  - building site
- Simple pieces of apparatus may have to be made for the game (such as spinners, special dice).
- The rules should be written out clearly for others to play the game.

Pupil Mastersheets A1 – 75
These sheets are for pupils to work on and record their findings in conjunction with given activities.

Appendix A

Nelson

MATHS BANK 3
LEVEL THREE

Number & Algebra

Nelson

MASTERSHEET A1

ACTIVITY

Name: _____ Date: _____ Teacher: _____

Use counters on this abacus.

Evaluation:
reads, writes and orders numbers to 1000;
knows that position of a digit indicates its value

Teacher's comment:

See Activities 6, 7, 8 (p.13)

Maths Bank: Level 3   Number   Page 109

MASTERSHEET A2

ACTIVITY

Name:_____ Date:_____ Teacher:_____

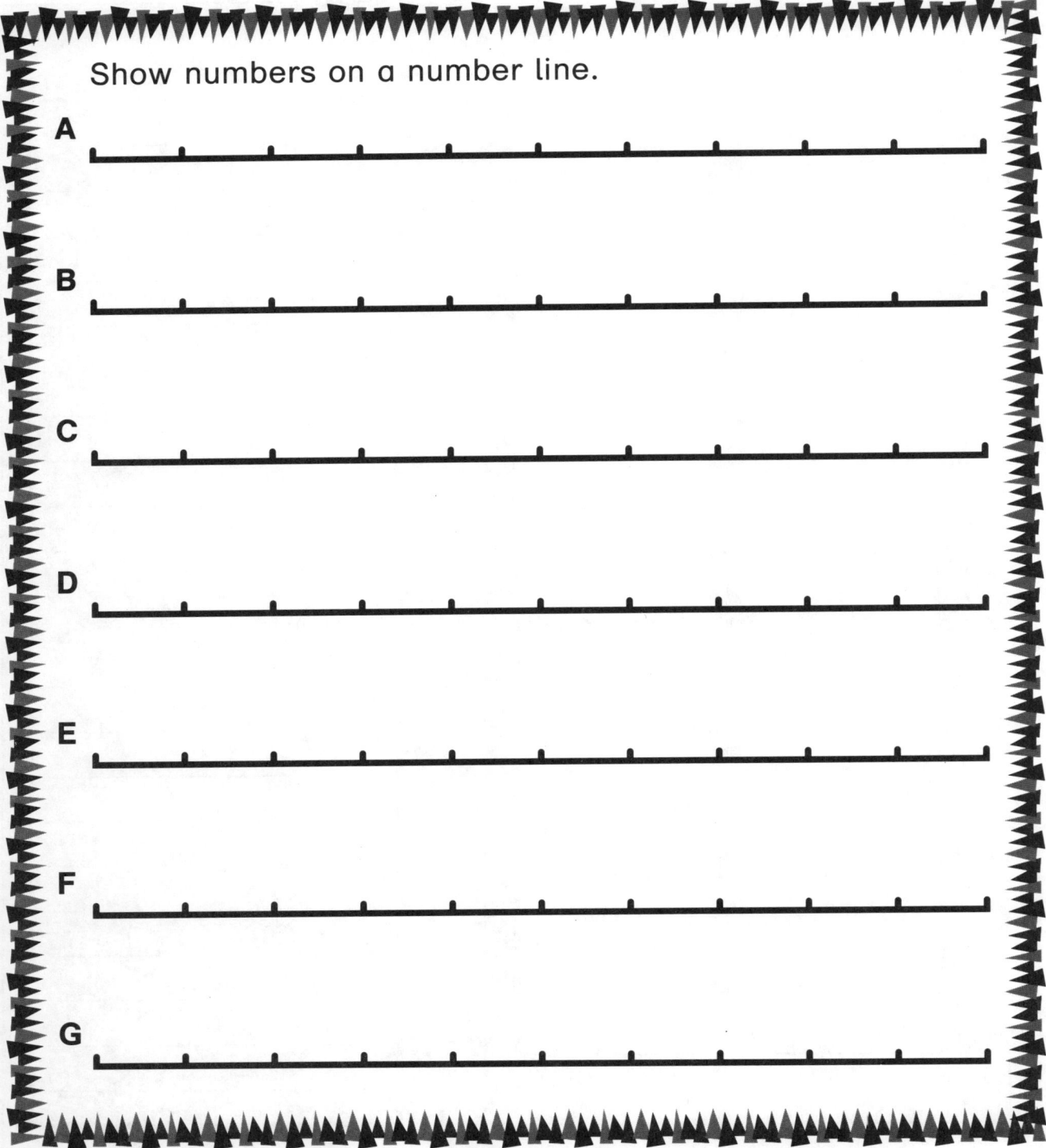

Show numbers on a number line.

A
B
C
D
E
F
G

Evaluation: *Teacher's comment:*

reads, writes and orders numbers to 1000;
knows that position of a digit indicates its value

See Activity 9 (p.14)

Number MATHS BANK: Level 3

MASTERSHEET A3

ACTIVITY

Name: _____ Date: _____ Teacher: _____

Show numbers on a number line.

A |‌‌‌|

B |‌‌‌|

C |‌‌‌|

D |‌‌‌|

E |‌‌‌|

F |‌‌‌|

G |‌‌‌|

Evaluation:

reads, writes and orders numbers to 1000;
know that position of a digit indicates its value

Teacher's comment:

See Activity 10 (p.15)

MATHS BANK: Level 3   Number   Page 111

MASTERSHEET A4

Name: _____ Date: _____ Teacher: _____

Show numbers on a number line.

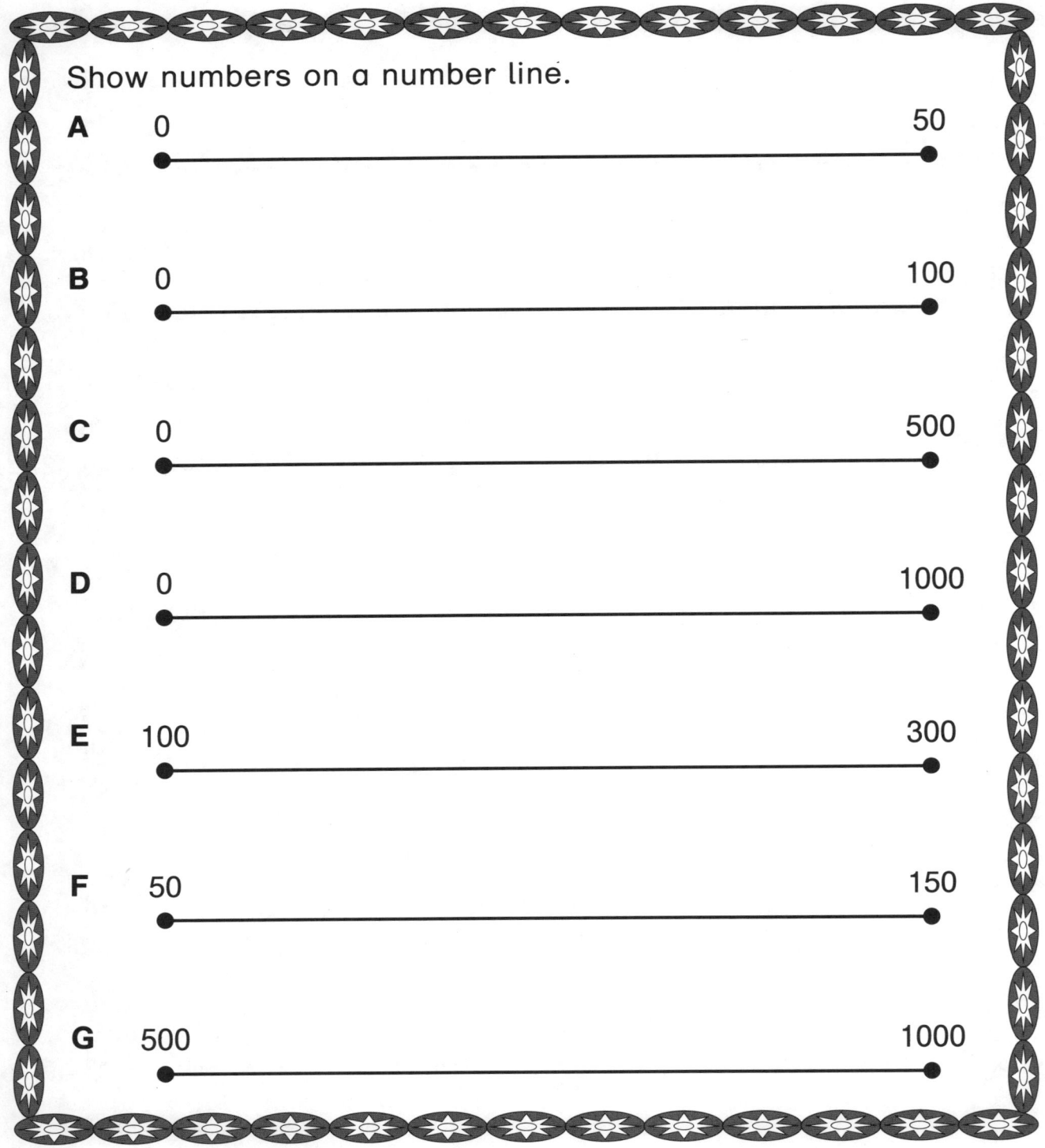

Evaluation:

able to approximate to nearest 10;
able to approximate to nearest 100;
able to estimate position on a number line

Teacher's comment:

See Activities 36, 37 (p.31)

MASTERSHEET A5

Name: _____ Date: _____ Teacher: _____

Write which numbers the base 10 apparatus is showing.

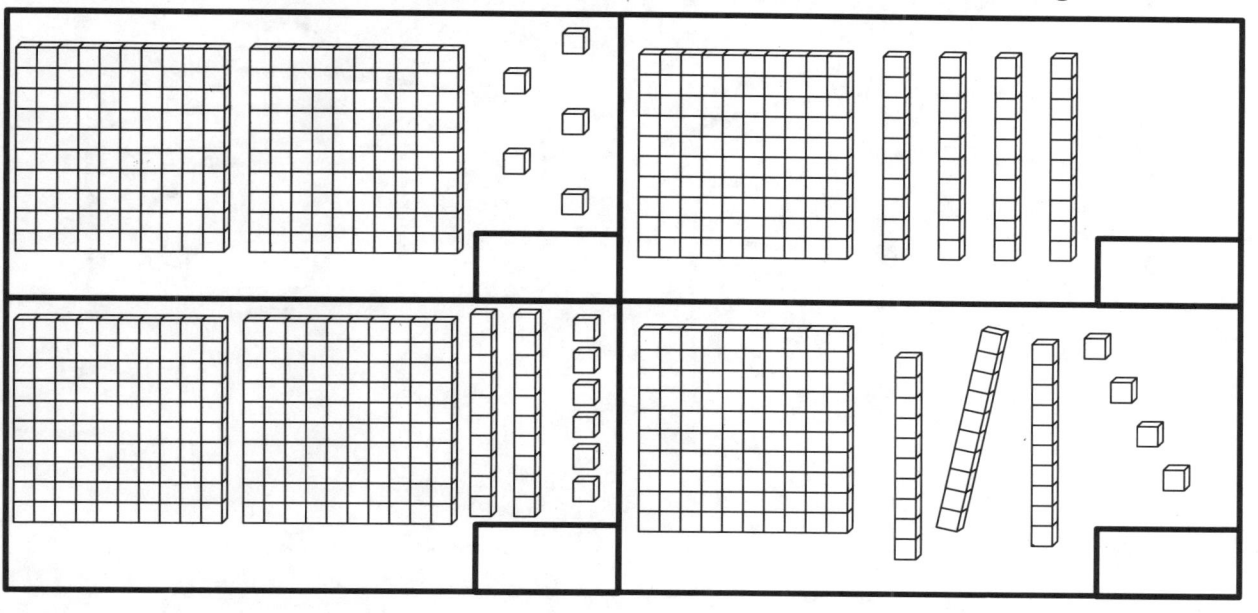

The base 10 apparatus is missing from each of these pictures. Draw it in.

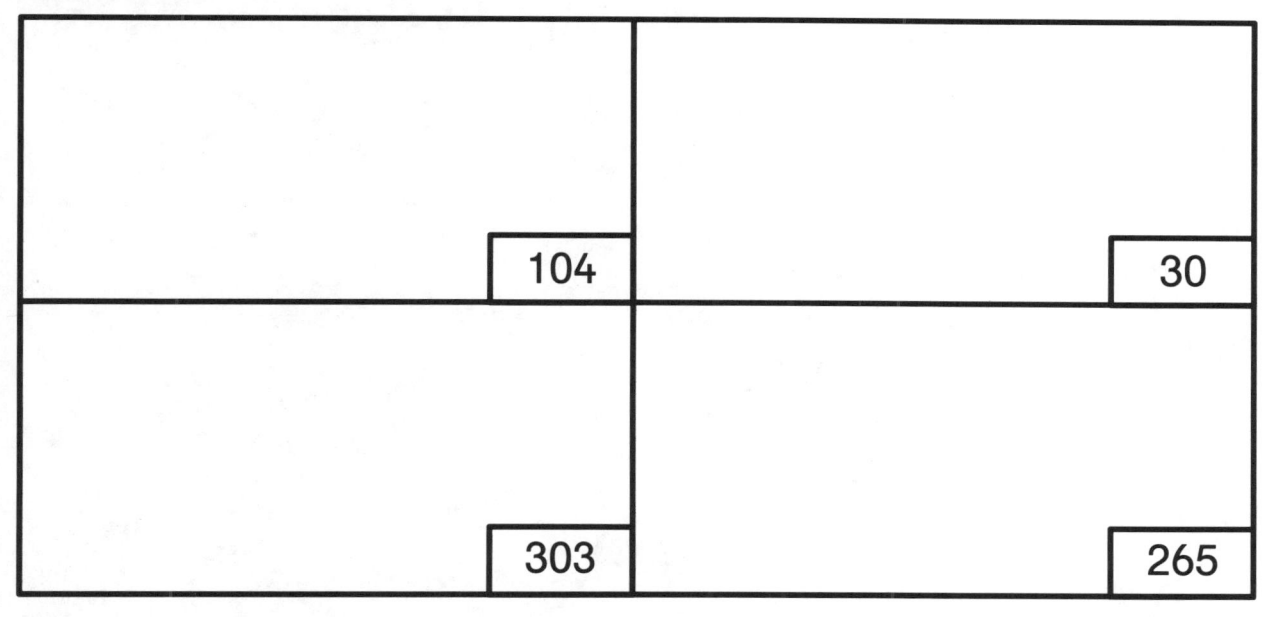

Evaluation:

reads, and records numbers to 1000;
knows that position of a digit indicates its value

Teacher's comment:

See Activity 12 (p.17)

MASTERSHEET A6

ACTIVITY

Name: _____ Date: _____ Teacher: _____

How much is there in each purse?

Evaluation:
able to record money using decimal notation;
uses money to aid calculations

Teacher's comment:

See Activity 13 (p.18)

Page 114   Number   MATHS BANK: Level 3

MASTERSHEET A7

Name: _____ Date: _____ Teacher: _____

Map pictures to correct purses.

Evaluation:

can use decimal notation to record money;
uses money to aid calculations;
can match coins to totals

Teacher's comment:

See Activity 14 (p.18)

MASTERSHEET A8

Name: _____ Date: _____ Teacher: _____

These calculator displays show some totals in pennies.
Write each total in pounds.

108.	450.	670.
544.	1200.	1378.
1050.	1425.	1005.

These calculator displays show some totals in pounds.
Write each total in pennies.

1.5	3.06	2.58
3.	10.8	13.2
15.08	17.	16.1

Evaluation:

able to use decimal notation to record money;
uses money to aid calculations;
able to represent money totals on a calculator

Teacher's comment:

See Activity 15 (p.18)

MATHS BANK : Level 3

MASTERSHEET A9

Name: _____ Date: _____ Teacher: _____

Write down the temperature each thermometer shows.

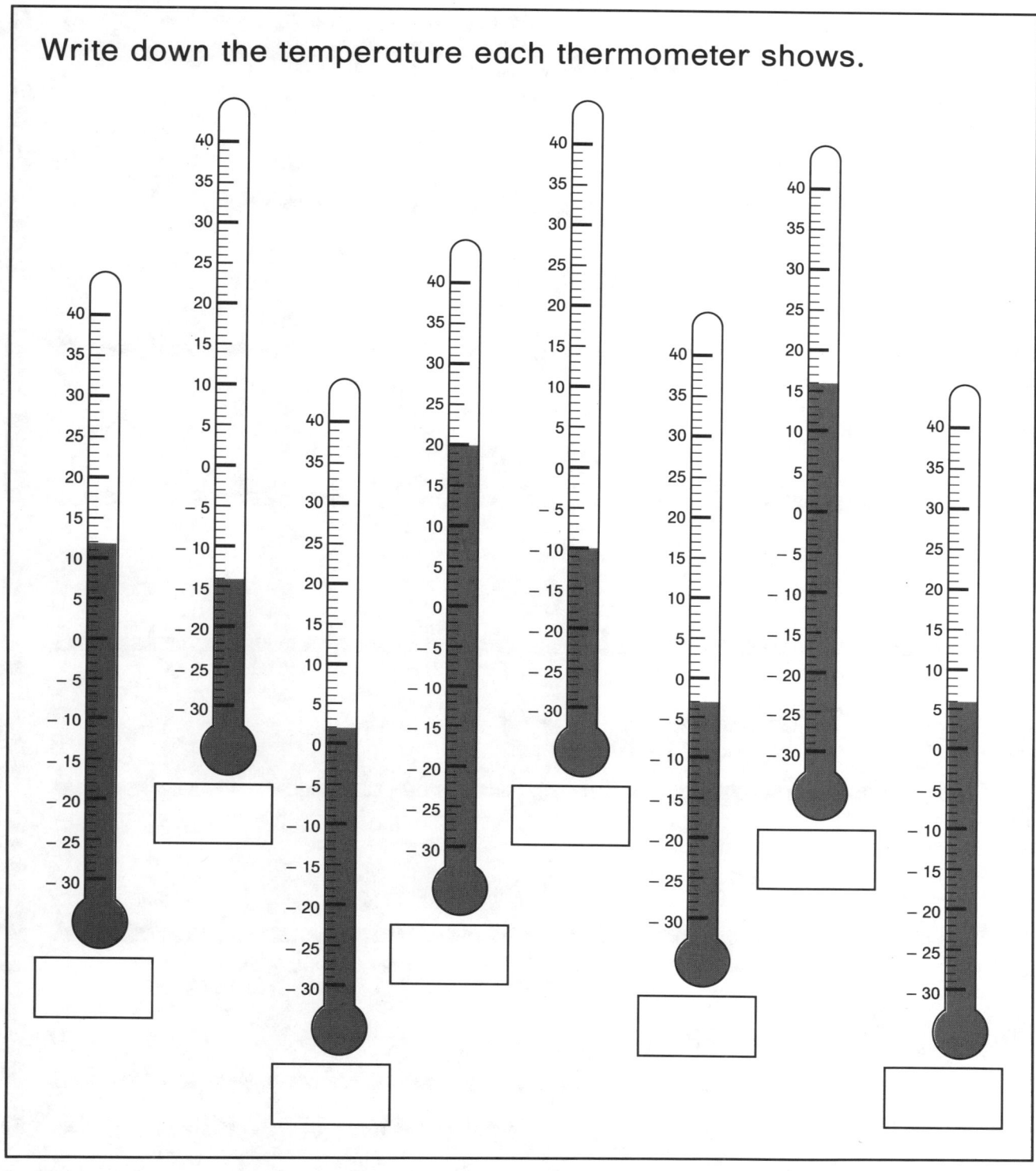

Evaluation:
able to interpret thermometer readings;
able to understand negative readings

Teacher's comment:

See Activity 16 (p.19)

MASTERSHEET A10

Name: _____ Date: _____ Teacher: _____

Which number does each arrow point to?

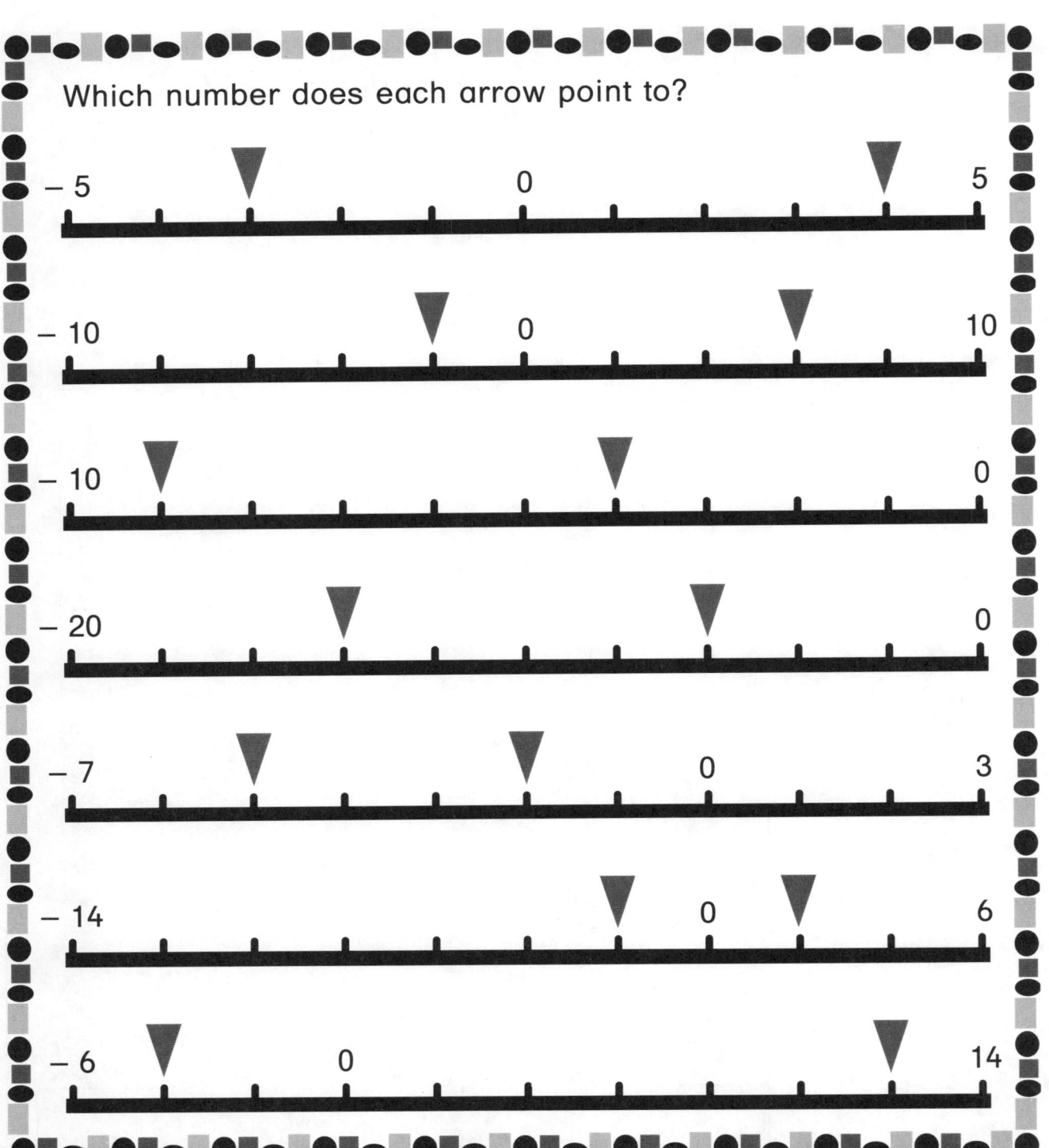

Evaluation: can understand negative readings

Teacher's comment:

See Activity 17 (p.19)

MASTERSHEET A11

ACTIVITY

Name: _____ Date: _____ Teacher: _____

Find the answers to each set of calculator touches.
Show what is happening on each number line.

5 − 8 = ☐

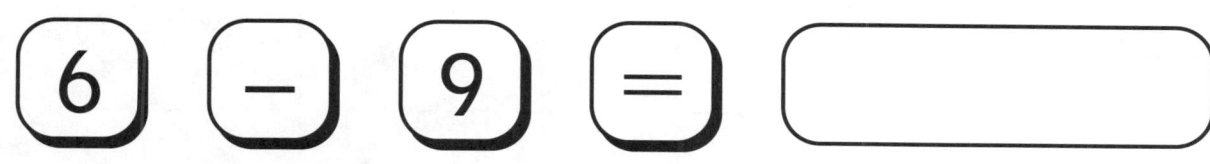

6 − 9 = ☐

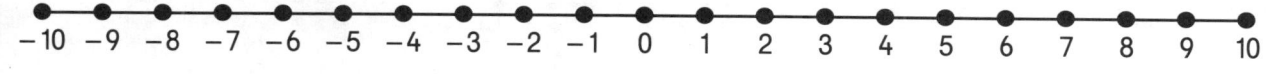

4 − 9 = ☐

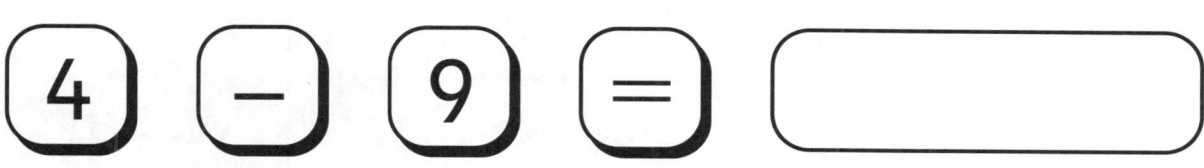

Evaluation:
understands negative output on a calculator;
understands negative numbers on a number line

Teacher's comment:

See Activity 18 (p.20)

MATHS BANK: Level 3   Number

MASTERSHEET A12

Name: _____ Date: _____ Teacher: _____

Digit grid

6	4	2	1	0	3	7	8
9	5	3	5	6	1	2	9
4	8	7	3	0	9	2	4
5	5	8	7	1	4	6	2
6	7	6	1	8	4	5	3
9	9	3	5	8	0	2	1
7	4	3	8	0	4	2	9
8	5	3	3	7	6	2	1
5	9	7	4	5	5	0	8
6	6	8	4	5	9	9	2

Evaluation:

knows addition and subtraction facts to 20

Teacher's comment:

See Activities 19, 20, 21, 22 (p.21 – 2)

MASTERSHEET A13

Name: _____ Date: _____ Teacher: _____

A   8 + 4

B   9 + 7

C   8 + 8

D   6 + 4

E   9 + 3

F   4 + 7

G   5 + 6

H   7 + 7

I   2 + 3 + 8

J   7 + 3 + 5

K   8 + 1 + 7

L   3 + 6 + 2

M   5 + 4

N
```
  8
+ 7
```

O
```
  4
  3
+ 9
```

P
```
  6
  9
+ 4
```

Evaluation:
knows addition facts to 20

Teacher's comment:

See Activity 23 (p.23)

MASTERSHEET A14

Name: _____ Date: _____ Teacher: _____

A 18 − 9	**G** 13 − 6	**M** 15 − 5
B 12 − 7	**H** 12 − 7	**N** $\begin{array}{r} 11 \\ -\ 7 \\ \hline \end{array}$
C 8 − 8	**I** 18 − 3 − 4	
D 16 − 8	**J** 17 − 3 − 4	**O** $\begin{array}{r} 13 \\ -\ 9 \\ \hline \end{array}$
E 17 − 7	**K** 14 − 1 − 7	
F 14 − 5	**L** 13 − 6 − 2	**P** $\begin{array}{r} 9 \\ -9 \\ \hline \end{array}$

Evaluation: knows subtraction facts to 20

Teacher's comment:

See Activity 24 (p.23)

MASTERSHEET A15

Name: _____ Date: _____ Teacher: _____

A 16 − 9

B 10 + 7

C 8 + 8

D 16 − 7

E 14 − 7

F 8 + 5

G 13 − 9

H 2 + 7

I 18 − 3 + 4

J 15 + 3 − 4

K 18 − 1 − 7

L 13 + 6 − 5

M 15 + 2 + 5

N 11 − 7 − 4

O 13 + 5 − 8

P 9 + 1 + 7

Evaluation:
knows addition and subtraction facts to 20

Teacher's comment:

See Activity 25 (p.24)

MASTERSHEET A16

Name: _____ Date: _____ Teacher: _____

What will be the date in one week's time?
....

Find the total cost of the following:

How much change would there be from 20p?
....

What is the total in this hand of cards?

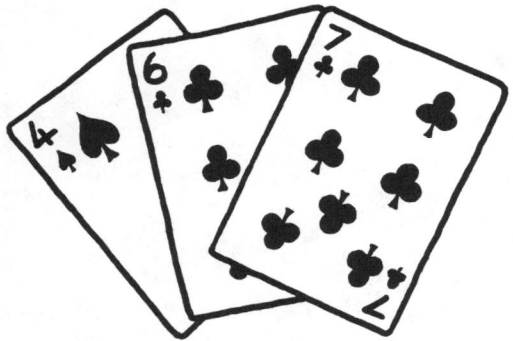

Which extra card is needed to make the total 20?
....

Which of these cards will make a total of 15?

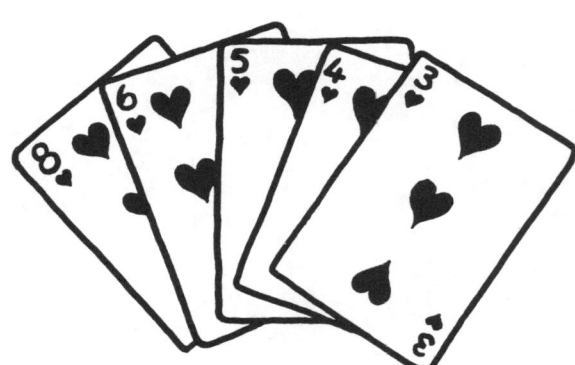

Which cards have a difference of 5?
....

Evaluation:
knows addition and subtraction facts to 20

Teacher's comment:

See Activity 26 (p.25)

MASTERSHEET A17

ACTIVITY

Name: _____ Date: _____ Teacher: _____

Write some number sentences for each set of numbers.

7, 4, 11

6, 8, 14

5, 10, 15

Choose your own set of three numbers.
Write number sentences for each set.

☐ ☐ ☐

☐ ☐ ☐

☐ ☐ ☐

Evaluation:
knows addition and subtraction trios to 20

Teacher's comment:

See Activity 27 (p.25)

MASTERSHEET A18

ACTIVITY

Name: _____ Date: _____ Teacher: _____

What would 4 audio tapes cost?

What would 3 video tapes cost?

What would one can of pop cost?

What would one battery cost?

Evaluation:

can solve multiplication problems;
can solve division problems

Teacher's comment:

See Activity 28 (p.26)

MASTERSHEET A19

Name: _____ Date: _____ Teacher: _____

Explain how to work out the answers to each of these problems.

A car travels 32 miles on one gallon of petrol.
How far will it travel on eight gallons of petrol?

_____

A car travels 1288 miles on 28 gallons of petrol.
How many miles per gallon did it do?

_____

One ounce is about the same as thirty grams.
How many ounces would be the same as 210 grams?

_____

There are 1760 yards in a mile.
How many yards are there in quarter of a mile?

_____

Evaluation:
can solve multiplication problems;
can solve division problems

Teacher's comment:

See Activity 29 (p.26)

MASTERSHEET A20

ACTIVITY

Name: _____ Date: _____ Teacher: _____

Join the pairs which have the same answer.

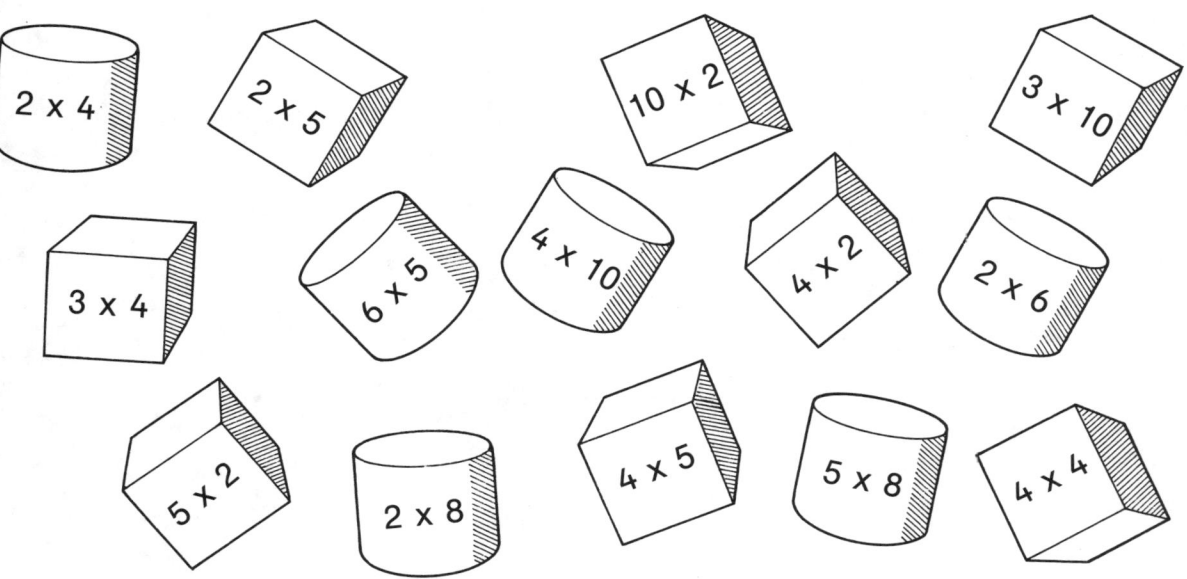

Write two multiplication facts for each number:

10    14

18   35

50   45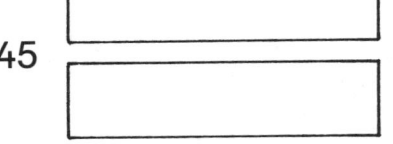

Evaluation:
knows multiplication facts to 5x5;
knows 2, 5, 10 multiplication tables;
understands that multiplication is commutative

Teacher's comment:

See Activity 32 (p.27)

MASTERSHEET A21

ACTIVITY

Name: _____ Date: _____ Teacher: _____

How many boxes will be needed for each set of eggs?
How many eggs will be in each partly filled box?

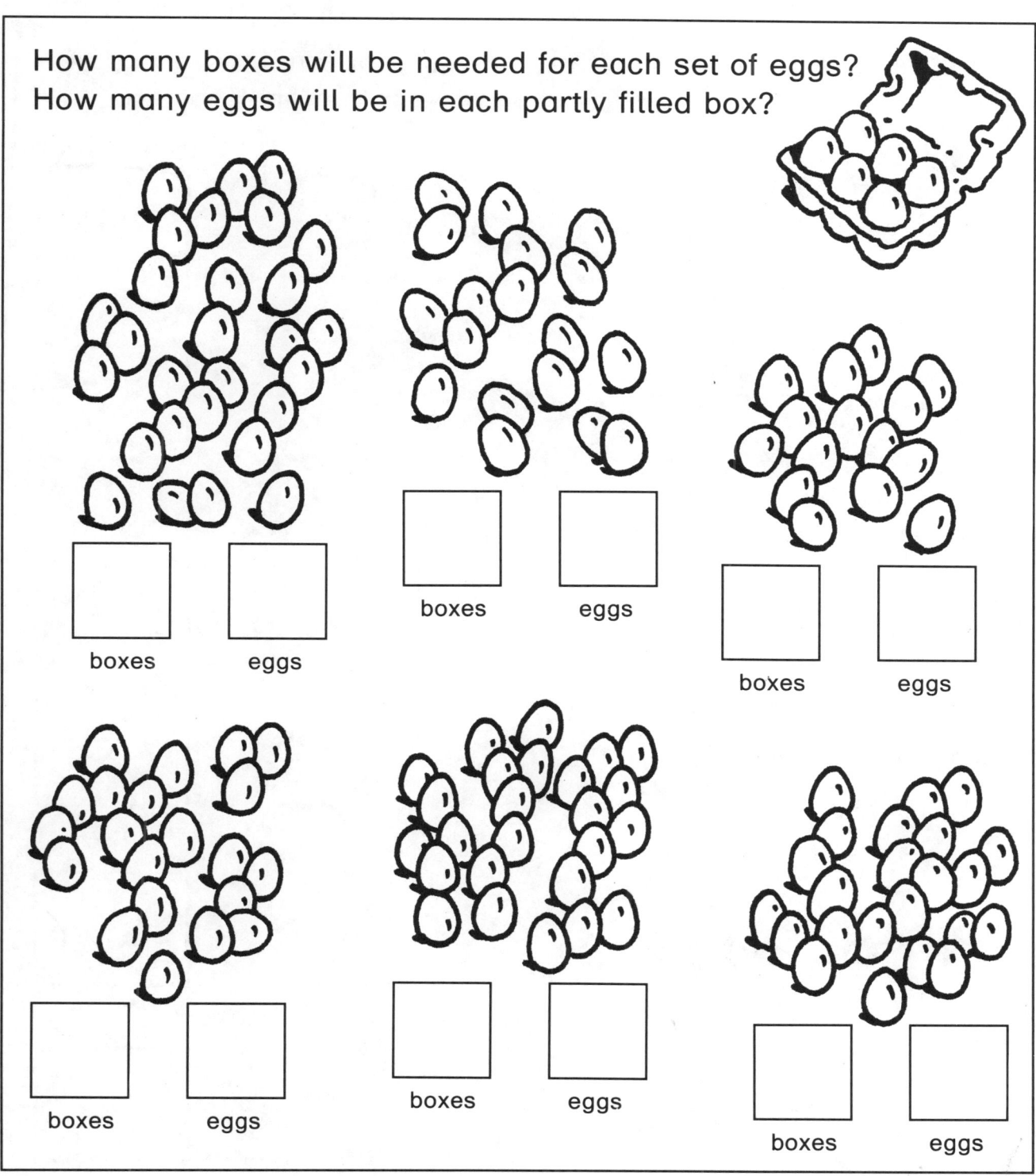

Evaluation:
understands remainders;
can round up

Teacher's comment:

See Activity 39 (p.33)

MATHS BANK: Level 3   Number   Page 129

MASTERSHEET A22

ACTIVITY

Name: _____ Date: _____ Teacher: _____

What are the next two numbers in each pattern?
Try to predict which number will come in the tenth position.

10th number

1 2 3 1 2 3 __ __ ...   [ ]

5 10 15 20 25 __ __ ...   [ ]

1 2 1 3 1 4 1 __ __ ...   [ ]

13 23 33 43 53 __ __ ...   [ ]

100 96 92 88 84 __ __ ...   [ ]

1 5 2 10 3 15 __ __ ...   [ ]

Evaluation:
able to explain number patterns;
able to predict numbers in patterns

Teacher's comment:

See Activity 43 (p.36)

Page 130 — Number/Algebra — MATHS BANK: Level 3

MASTERSHEET A23

ACTIVITY

Name: _____ Date: _____ Teacher: _____

Number Grid A

10	9	8	7	6	5	4	3	2	1
			17				13		
					25				
		38							31
	49					44			
					56				
					66			62	
									71
100									

Number Grid B

	99			95			92		
									90
			77						
						67			70
						54			
41									
	39					34			
21									30
	19								
1	2	3	4	5	6	7	8	9	10

Evaluation:
able to explain number patterns;
able to predict numbers in patterns

Teacher's comment:

See Activities 44, 45 (pp.37 – 8)

MATHS BANK: Level 3   Number/Algebra   Page 131

MASTERSHEET A24

ACTIVITY

Name: _____ Date: _____ Teacher: _____

Number Grid C

	12				17		
	45			49			
8	70				75		21
		89					
	39					56	
3				82			
				60			
1					30		

Number Grid D

		31		28			
	60		3	2	9		78
				1			
		16				45	
	37						
				69			

Evaluation:
able to explain number patterns;
able to predict numbers in patterns

Teacher's comment:

See Activities 44, 45 (pp.37 – 8)

Number/Algebra   MATHS BANK: Level 3

MASTERSHEET A25

ACTIVITY

Name: _____ Date: _____ Teacher: _____

Find several ways of writing each of these numbers.

34   **47**   **59**

67   **78**   **91**

Evaluation: *Teacher's comment:*

can express 2-digit numbers in equivalent forms

See Activity 46 (p.39)

MASTERSHEET A26

Name: _____ Date: _____ Teacher: _____

Digit card games

Results

Evaluation:
recognises numbers which are divisible by 2, 5 and 10

Teacher's comment:

See Activity 49 (p.41)

Page 134 — Number/Algebra — Maths Bank: Level 3

MASTERSHEET A27

ACTIVITY

Name: _____ Date: _____ Teacher: _____

Roll two dice to make 2-digit numbers.
Write the numbers on the diagram.

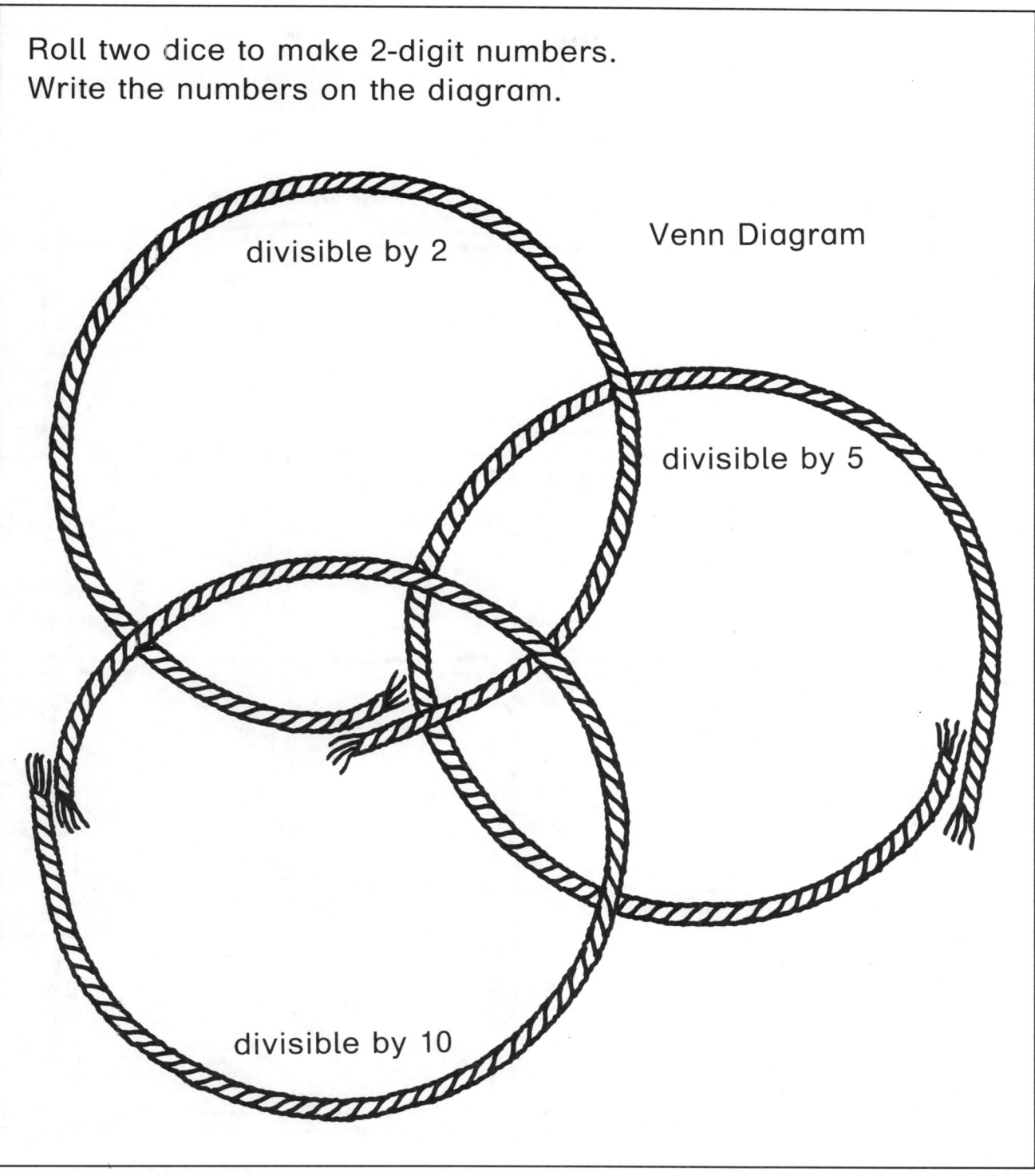

Venn Diagram

divisible by 2

divisible by 5

divisible by 10

Evaluation:

recognises numbers which are divisible by 2;
recognises numbers which are divisible by 5;
recognises numbers which are divisible by 10

Teacher's comment:

See Activity 50 (p.42)

MASTERSHEET A28

Name: _____ Date: _____ Teacher: _____

Roll two dice to make 2-digit numbers.
Write the numbers on the diagram.

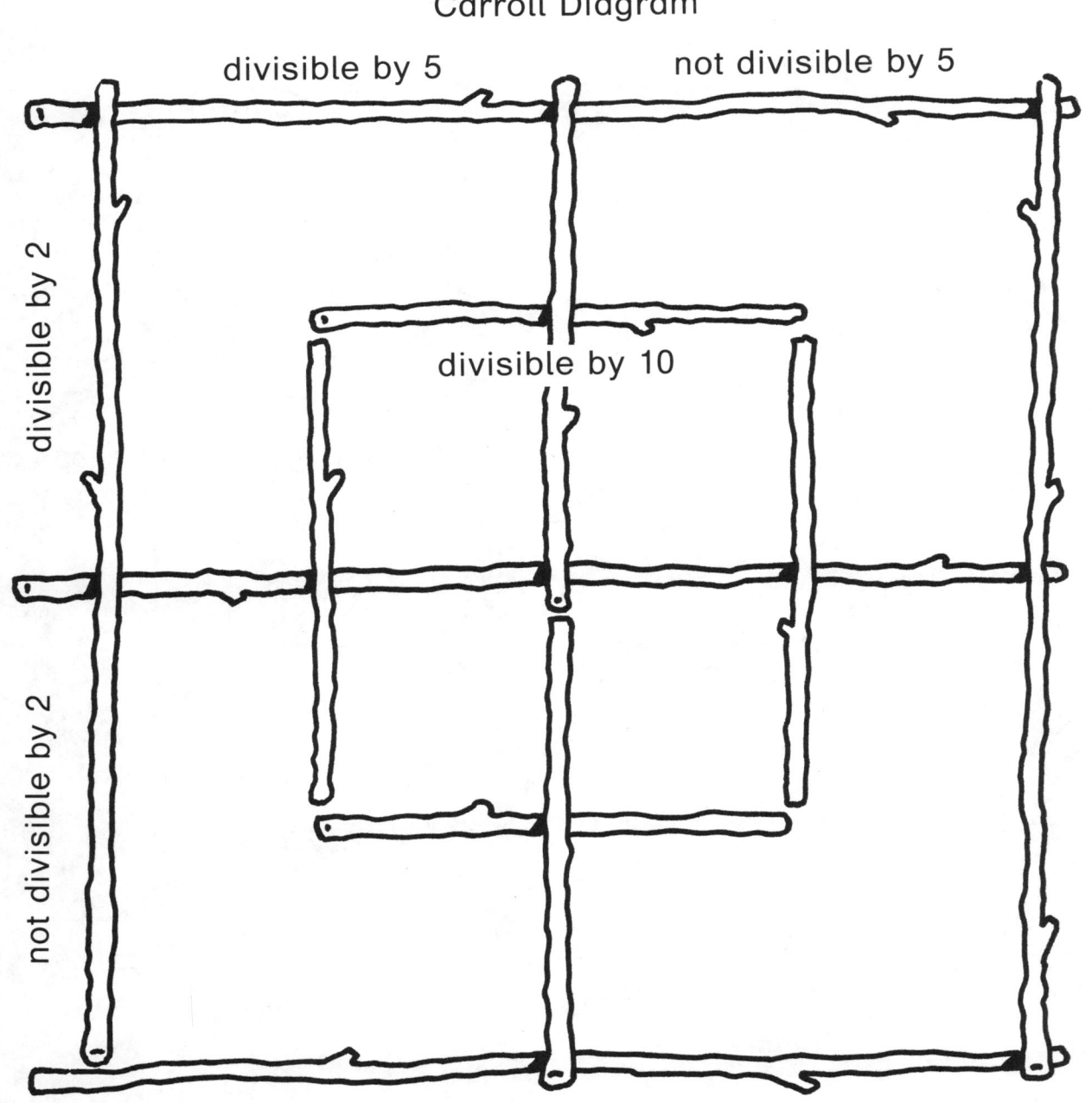

Evaluation:

recognises numbers which are divisible by 2;
recognises numbers which are divisible by 5;
recognises numbers which are divisible by 10

Teacher's comment:

See Activity 51 (p.42)

MASTERSHEET A29

Name:_____ Date:_____ Teacher:_____

What is the output from each of these machines?
Write the numbers in the correct order in the spaces.

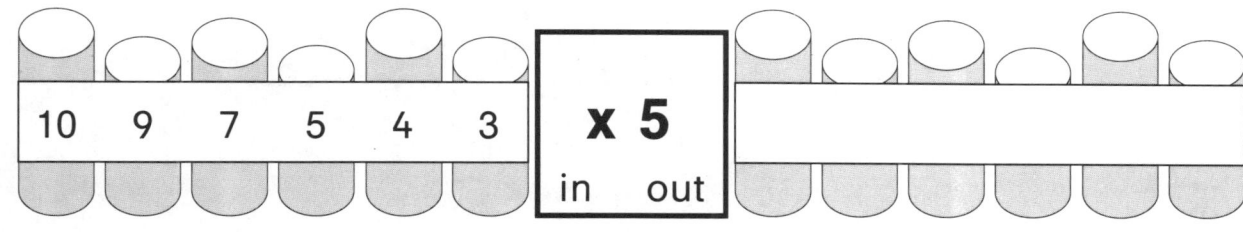

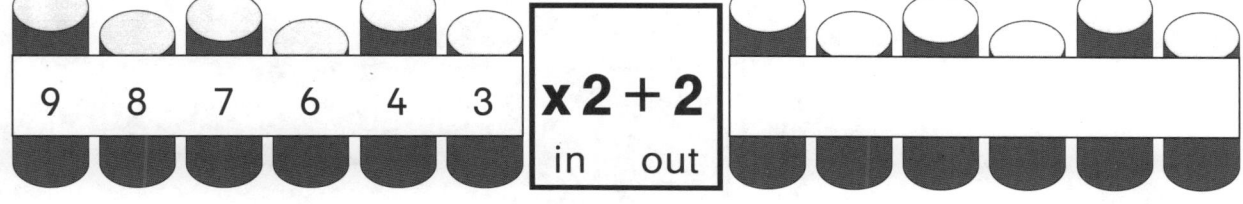

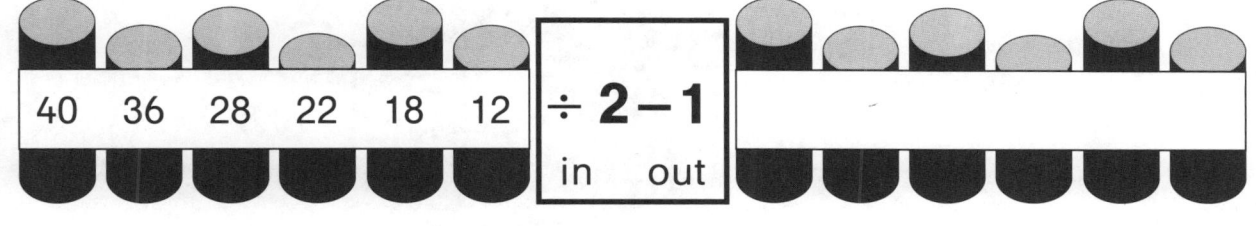

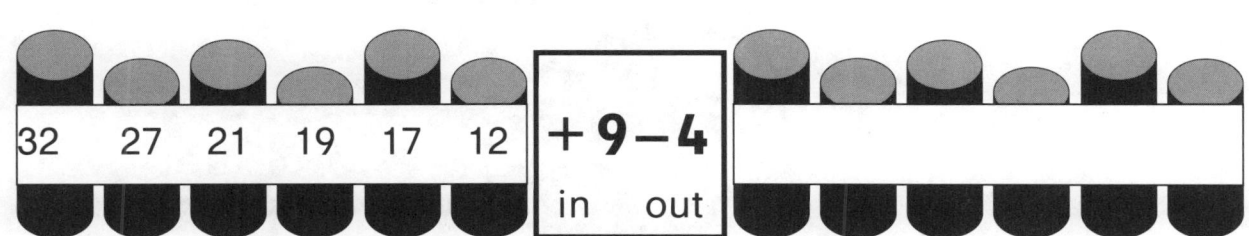

Evaluation: Teacher's comment:

can calculate outputs from simple function machines

See Activity 52 (p.43)

MASTERSHEET A30

Name: _____ Date: _____ Teacher: _____

ACTIVITY

What is the input for each of these machines?
Write the numbers in the correct order in the spaces.

in | +9 | out 32 25 17 14 11 9

in | −10 | out 87 75 62 58 44 31

in | ×10 | out 100 80 70 50 40 30

in | ÷2 | out 10 8 7 6 5 3

in | +5 −2 | out 21 19 17 16 13 8

Evaluation: *Teacher's comment:*

can calculate inputs for simple function machines

See Activity 53 (p.43)

Page 138 Algebra Maths Bank : Level 3

MASTERSHEET A31

Name: _____ Date: _____ Teacher: _____

What is each of these machines doing to the numbers?

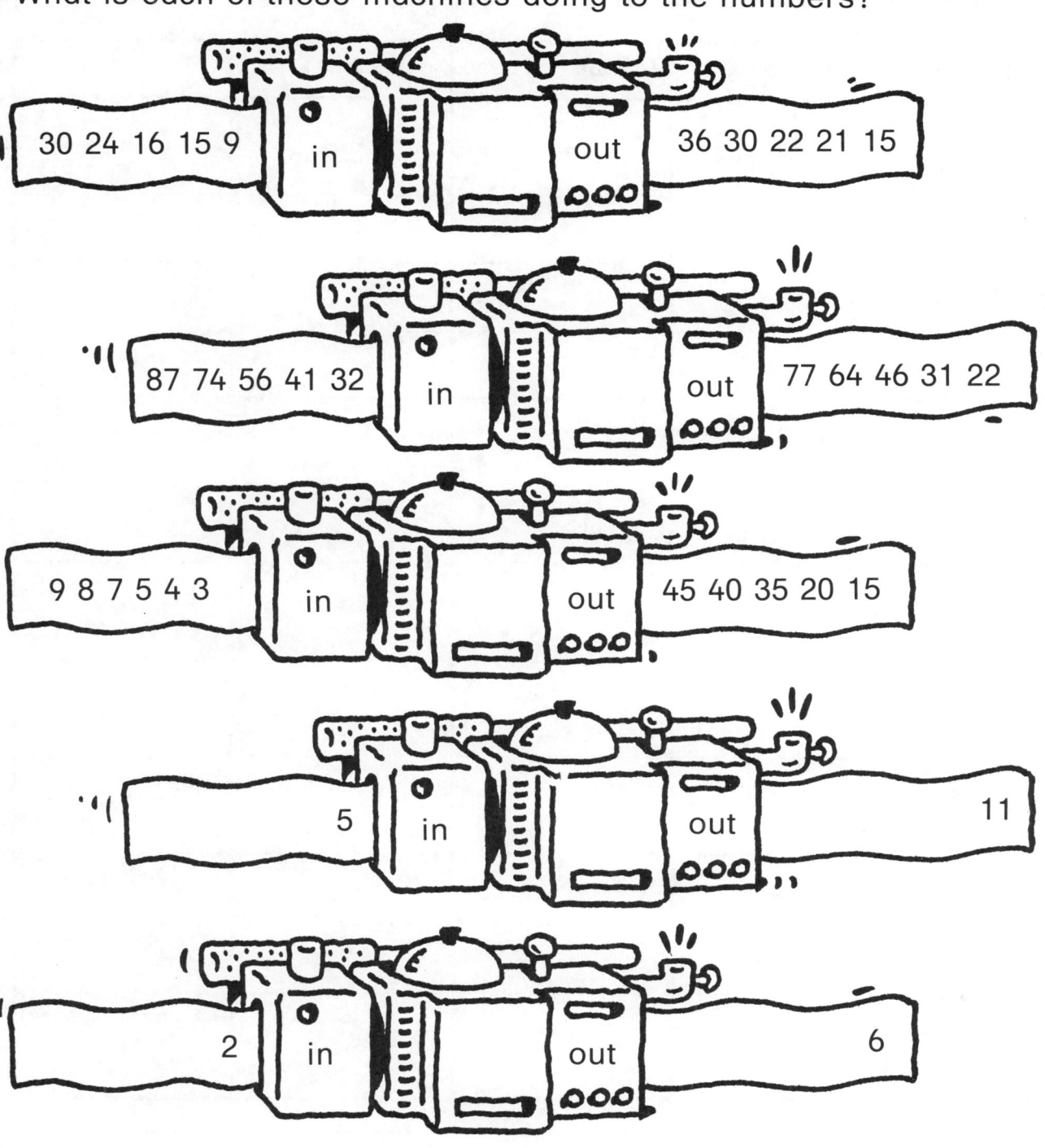

Evaluation:
can work out functions given input and output

Teacher's comment:

See Activity 54 (p.44)

MASTERSHEET A32

ACTIVITY

Name: _____ Date: _____ Teacher: _____

Measure each of these items:

Item to be measured	Instrument used	Estimate	Measurement
Perimeter of wastepaper container			
Gap under a door			
Length of playground			
Your hand span			
Diameter of a tin			
Weight of a house brick			
Weight of 30 Multilink cubes			
Temperature of water from the cold tap			
Temperature of the classroom			
Capacity of a cup			
Capacity of a jug			
Time to write name and address neatly			

Evaluation:

chooses appropriate measuring instrument for task in hand;
can interpret numbers on a wide range of measuring instruments

Teacher's comment:

See Activity 67 (p.55)

MATHS BANK

LEVEL THREE

Measures

Nelson

MASTERSHEET A34

ACTIVITY

Name: _____ Date: _____ Teacher: _____

The units of measurement are missing from each of these pictures. Write in what you think each unit of measurement should be.

Height = 194 _____

Capacity = 15 _____

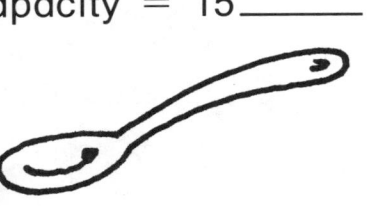

Capacity = 75 _____

Weight = 58 _____

Distance = 105 _____

Weight = 450 _____

Evaluation:
understands appropriate units of measurement

Teacher's comment:

See Activity 69 (p.56)

Measures

MATHS BANK 3
LEVEL THREE

Shape & space

Nelson

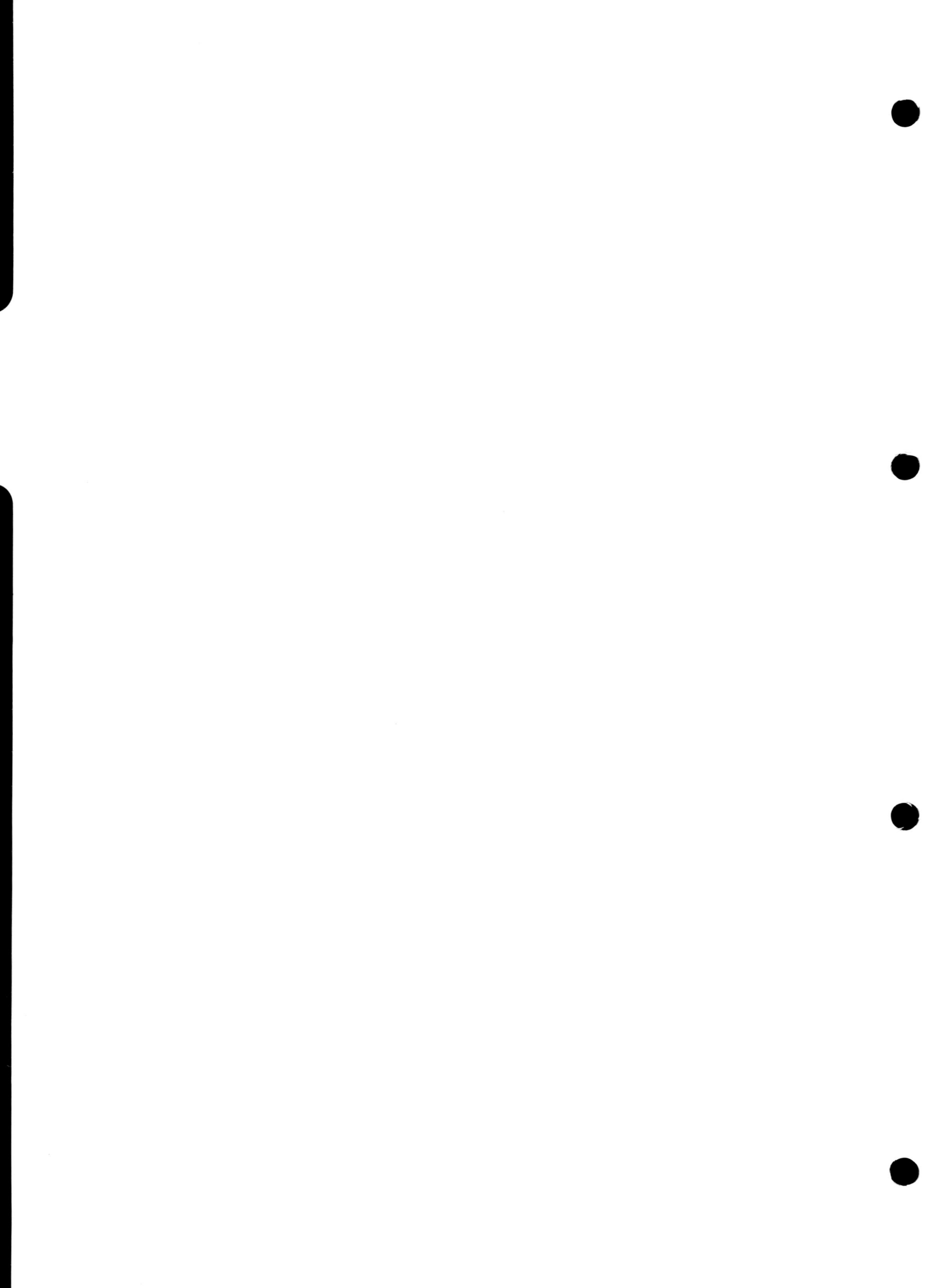

MASTERSHEET A35

ACTIVITY

Name: _____ Date: _____ Teacher: _____

Sort these shapes into sets.
Use colour to show which set each shape belongs to.

Colour of set	Reason for the sort

Evaluation:
able to sort 2–D shapes in different ways;
able to describe 2-D shapes accurately

Teacher's comment:

See Activity 77 (p.63)

Maths Bank: Level 3   Shape and space   Page 143

MASTERSHEET A36

ACTIVITY

Name: _____ Date: _____ Teacher: _____

Sort these shapes into sets.
Use colour to show which set each shape belongs to.

Colour of set	Reason for the sort

Evaluation:
able to sort 2-D shapes in different ways;
able to describe 2-D shapes accurately

Teacher's comment:

See Activity 78 (p.63)

Shape and space

MATHS BANK: Level 3

MASTERSHEET A37

ACTIVITY

Name: _____ Date: _____ Teacher: _____

Sort these shapes into sets.
Use colour to show which set each shape belongs to.

Colour of set	Reason for the sort

Evaluation:
able to sort 2-D shapes in different ways;
able to describe 2-D shapes accurately

Teacher's comment:

See Activity 79 (p.64)

Maths Bank: Level 3   Shape and space   Page 145

MASTERSHEET A38

ACTIVITY

Name: _____ Date: _____ Teacher: _____

Sort these shapes into sets.
Use colour to show which set each shape belongs to.

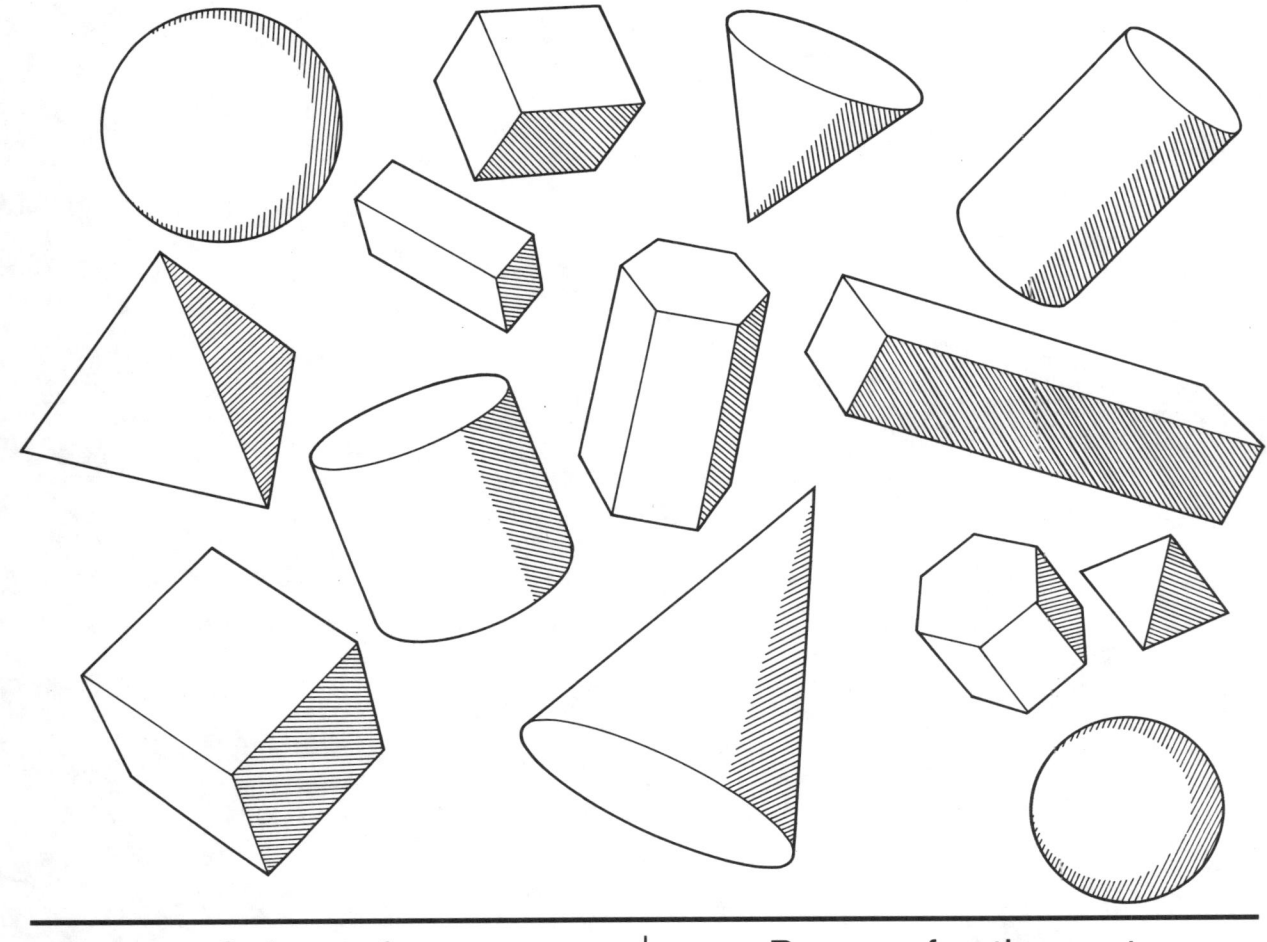

Colour of set	Reason for the sort

Evaluation:
can sort 3-D shapes in different ways;
can describe 3-D shapes accurately

Teacher's comment:

See Activity 80 (p.65)

Page 146 — Shape and space — MATHS BANK: Level 3

MASTERSHEET A39

ACTIVITY

Name: _____ Date: _____ Teacher: _____

Sort these shapes into sets.
Use colour to show which set each shape belongs to.

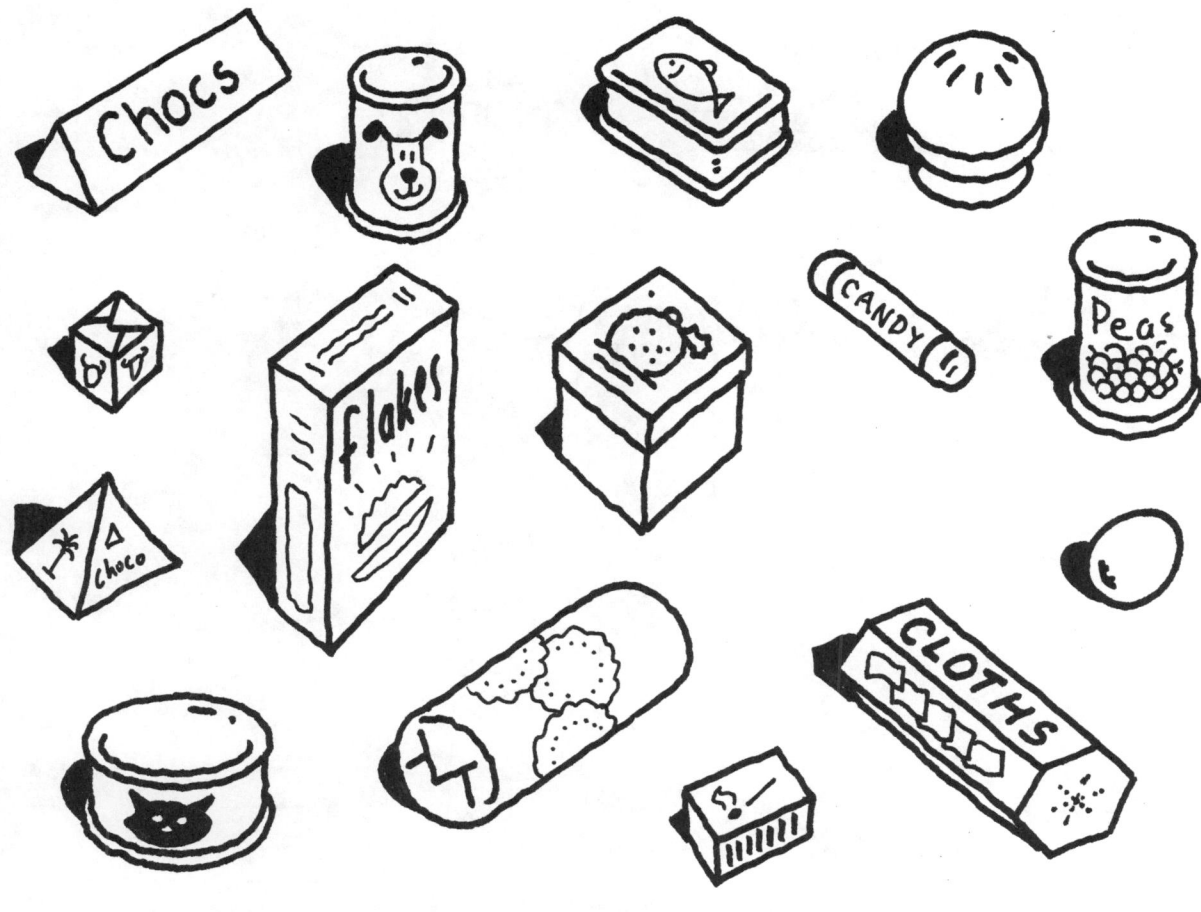

Colour of set	Reason for the sort

Evaluation:

can sort 3-D shapes in different ways;
can describe 3-D shapes accurately

Teacher's comment:

See Activity 81 (p.65)

Maths Bank : Level 3   Shape and space   Page 147

MASTERSHEET A40

ACTIVITY

Name: _____ Date: _____ Teacher: _____

Sort these shapes into sets.
Use colour to show which set each shape belongs to.

Colour of set	Reason for the sort

Evaluation:
sort 3-D shapes in different ways;
describe 3-D shapes accurately

Teacher's comment:

See Activity 82 (p.66)

Page 148   Shape and space   MATHS BANK: Level 3

MASTERSHEET A41

ACTIVITY

Name: _____ Date: _____ Teacher: _____

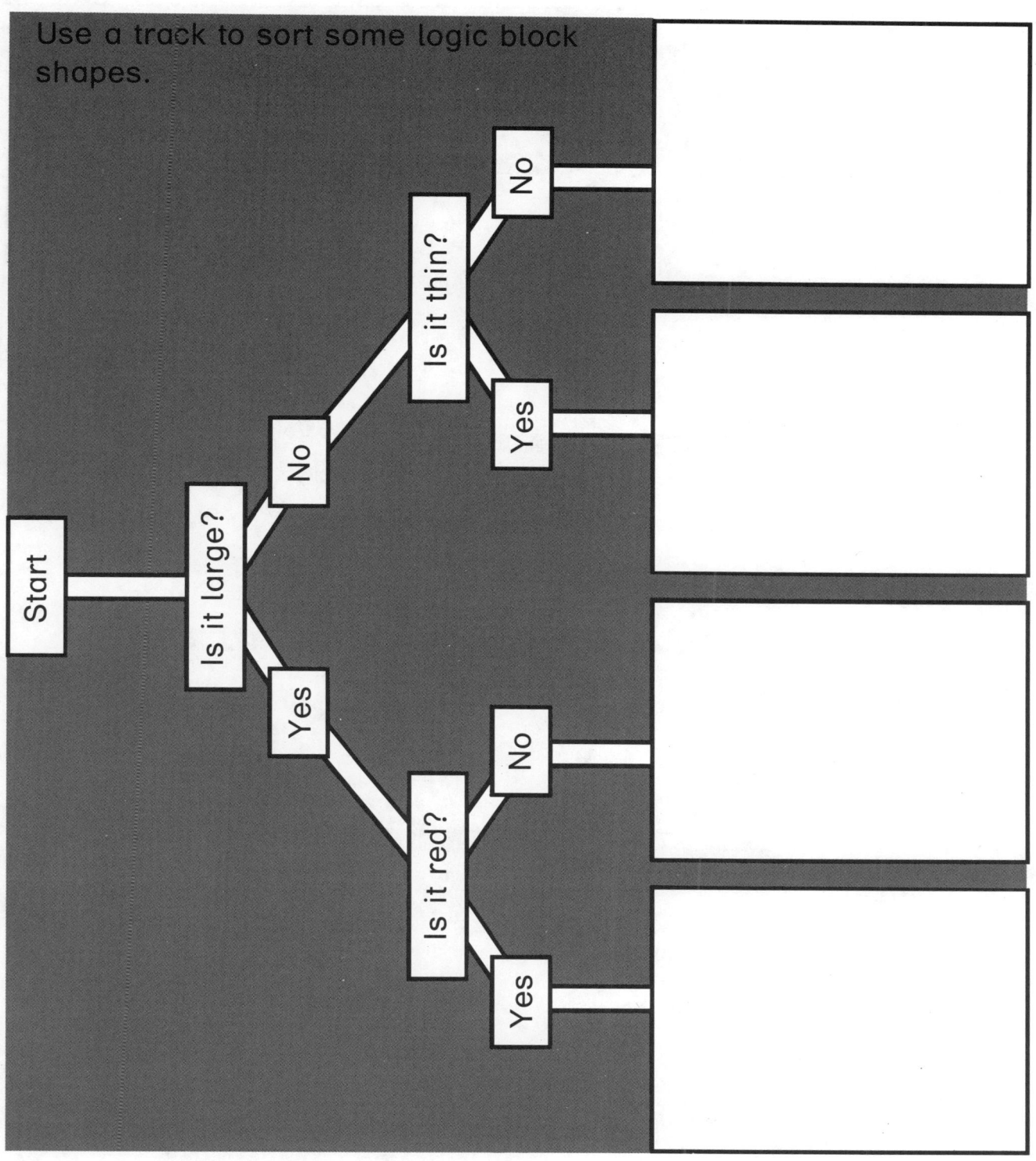

Use a track to sort some logic block shapes.

Evaluation:
able to sort 3-D shapes in different ways;
able to describe 3-D shapes accurately;
able to use a decision tree

Teacher's comment:

See Activity 84 (p.67)

MATHS BANK: Level 3 — Shape and space

MASTERSHEET A42

ACTIVITY

Name: _____ Date: _____ Teacher: _____

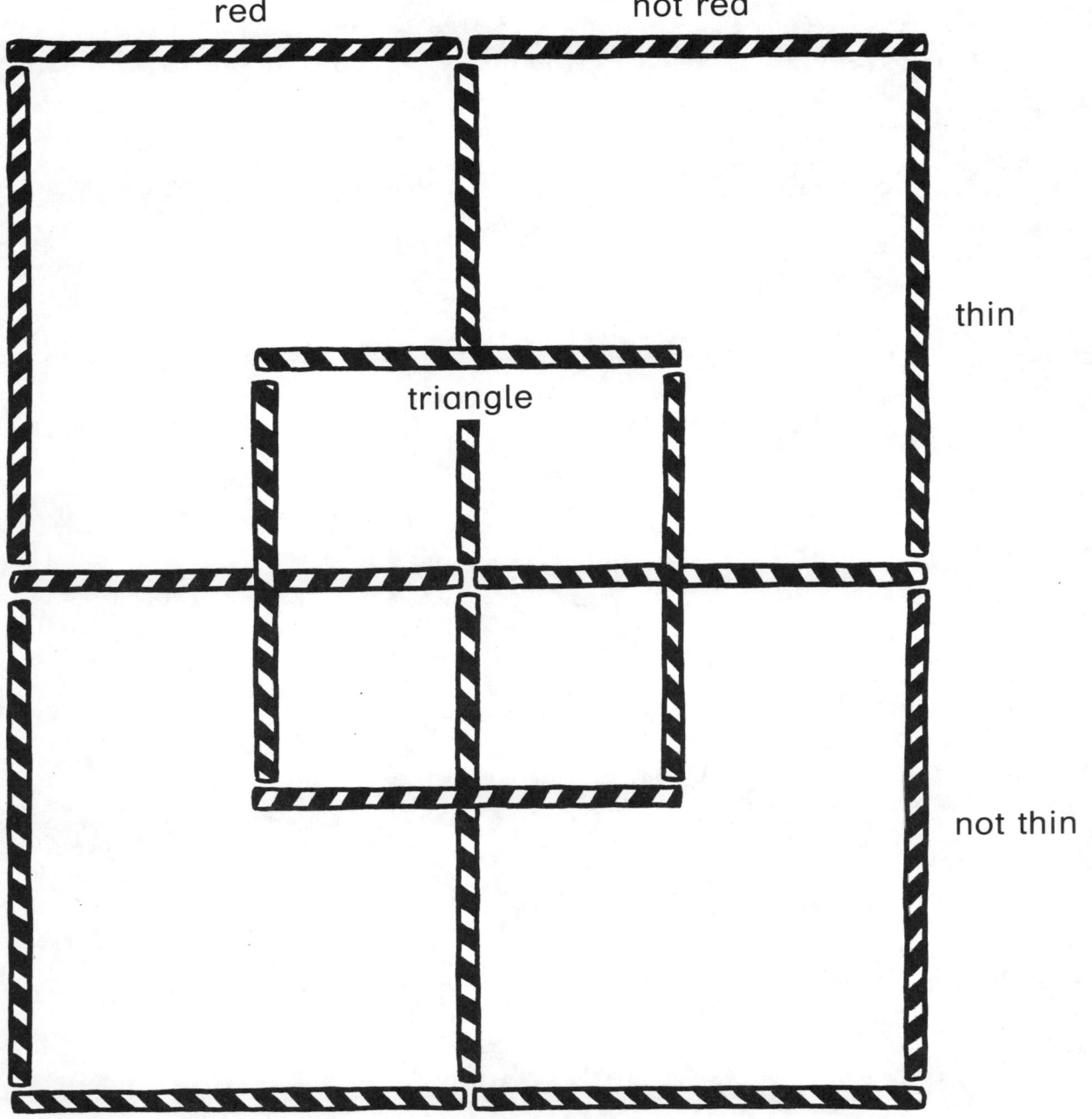

Sort some logic block shapes onto a Carroll diagram.

Evaluation:
able to sort 3-D shapes in different ways;
able to describe 3-D shapes accurately;
able to use a Carroll diagram

Teacher's comment:

See Activity 85 (p.68)

Page 150 Shape and space **Maths Bank : Level 3**

MASTERSHEET A43

ACTIVITY

Name: _____ Date: _____ Teacher: _____

Sort some logic block shapes onto a Venn diagram.

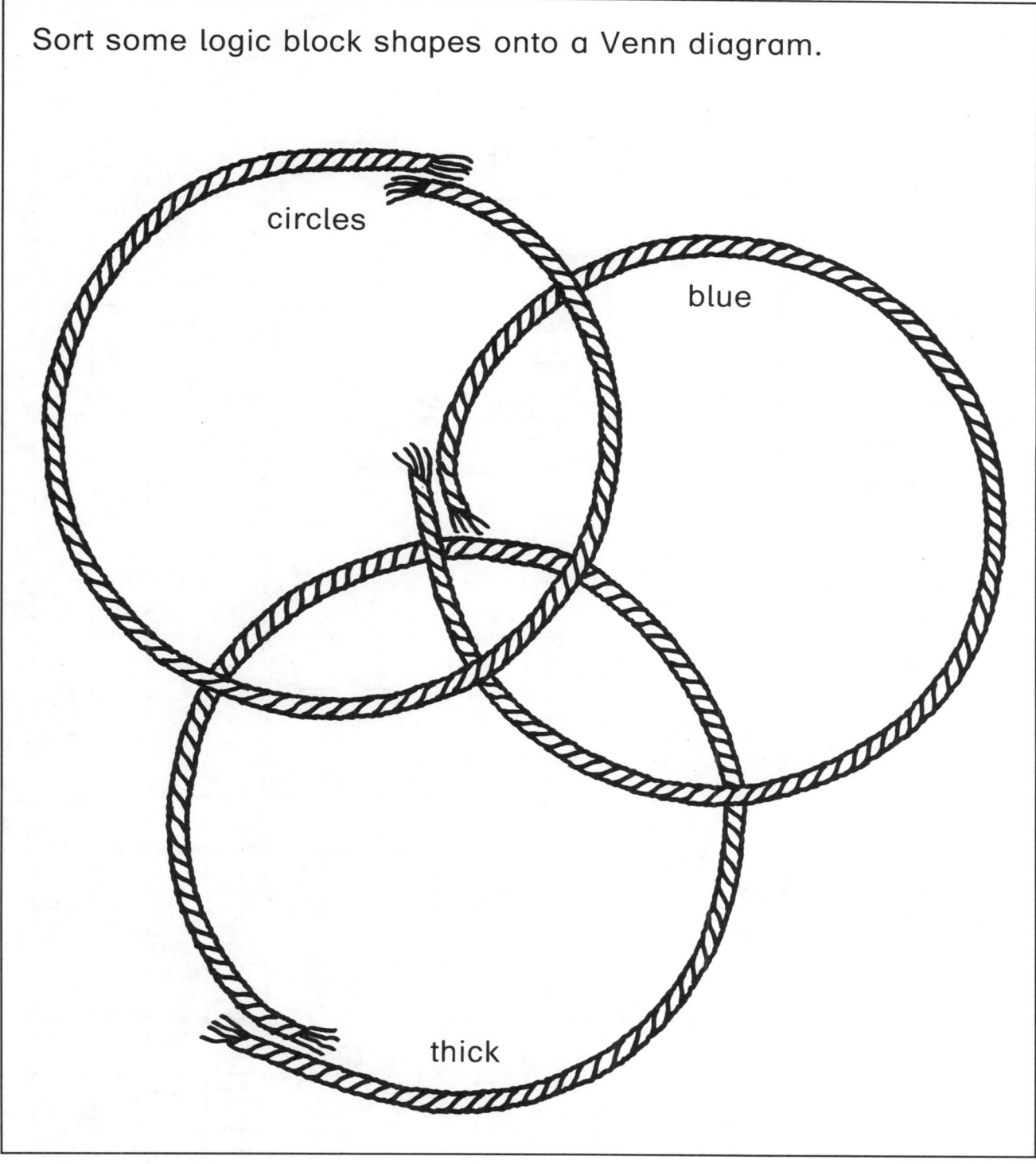

Evaluation:

able to sort 3-D shapes in different ways;
able to describe 3-D shapes accurately;
able to use a Venn diagram

Teacher's comment:

See Activity 86 (p.68)

MATHS BANK: Level 3 Shape and space Page 151

MASTERSHEET A44

ACTIVITY

Name: _____ Date: _____ Teacher: _____

Finish each picture to make it symmetrical.

Evaluation:
able to draw symmetrical shapes in 2-D

Teacher's comment:

See Activity 90 (p.71)

Page 152   Shape and space   MATHS BANK: Level 3

MASTERSHEET A45

ACTIVITY

Name: _____ Date: _____ Teacher: _____

Draw lines of symmetry on those shapes which are symmetrical.

Evaluation: *Teacher's comment:*
able to show lines of symmetry on simple shapes

See Activity 91 (p.71)

MATHS BANK: Level 3   Shape and space   Page 153

MASTERSHEET A46

ACTIVITY

Name: _____ Date: _____ Teacher: _____

Finish drawing this picture.
Everything you draw must have a line of symmetry.

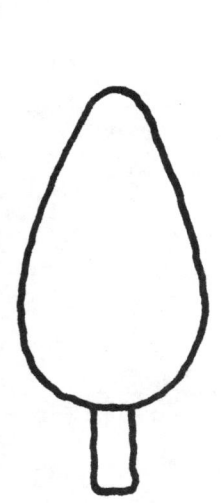  

Evaluation:
able to draw simple symmetrical shapes

Teacher's comment:

See Activity 92 (p.72)

Page 154 Shape and space **Maths Bank: Level 3**

MASTERSHEET A47

Name:_____ Date:_____ Teacher:_____

Make shapes on a geoboard.
Copy some of the shapes here.

Evaluation:
can make symmetrical patterns;
can make symmetrical shapes

Teacher's comment:

See Activity 94 (p.73)

Shape and space

MASTERSHEET A48

ACTIVITY

Name: _____ Date: _____ Teacher: _____

Record where you are standing.
Write something that you can see at each of the eight points of the compass.

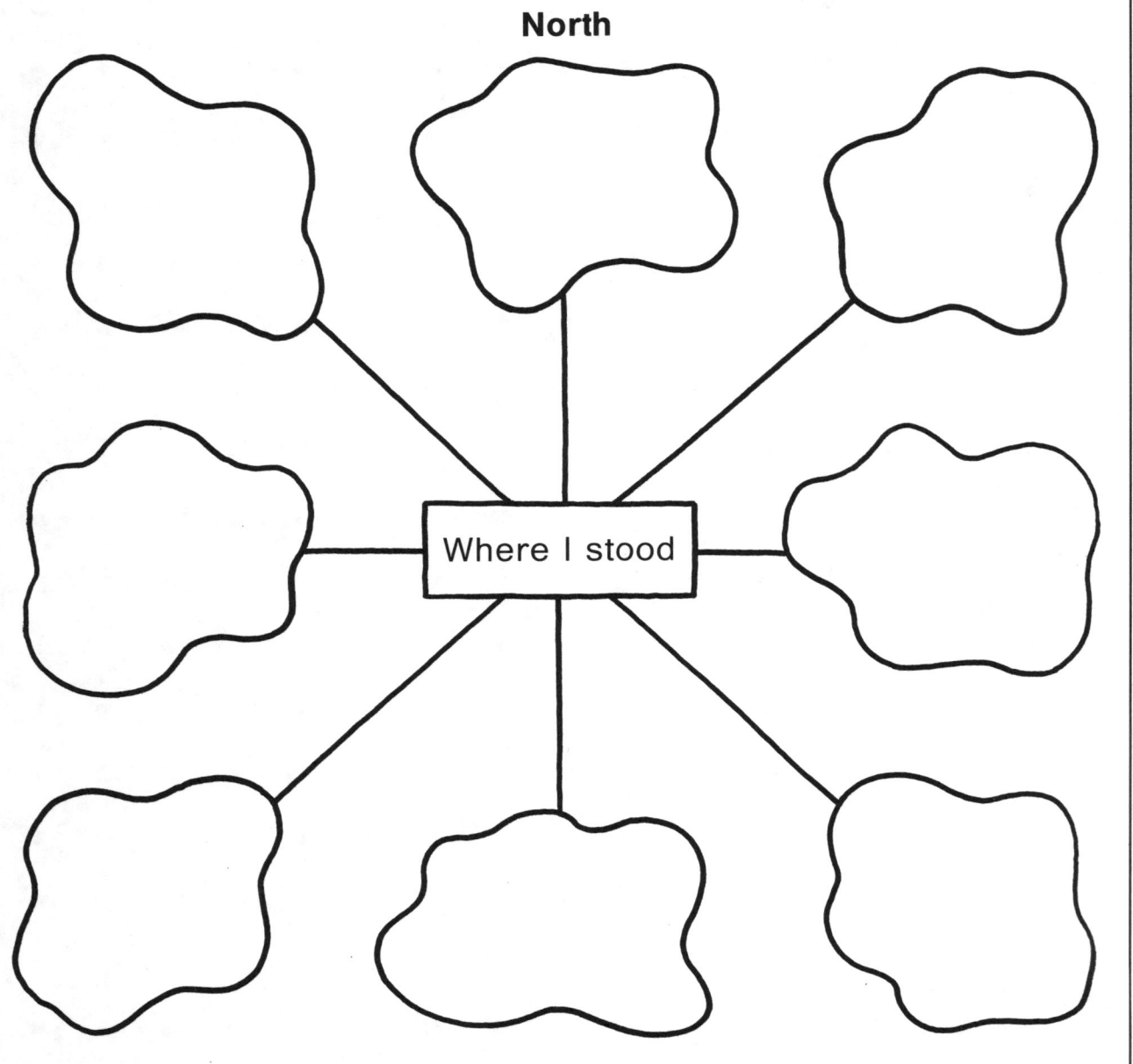

Evaluation:

knows eight points of the compass;
knows clockwise and anticlockwise

Teacher's comment:

See Activity 98 (p.75)

Shape and space

MATHS BANK: Level 3

MASTERSHEET A49

ACTIVITY

Name: _____ Date: _____ Teacher: _____

What is the main thing that the person in the picture sees if she turns:

East _____   South-West _____

West _____   North-West _____

What will she see if she turns a quarter turn clockwise having faced:

North _____   South-East _____

South _____   North-West _____

Evaluation:
knows eight points of the compass;
knows clockwise and anticlockwise

Teacher's comment:

See Activity 99 (p.76)

MATHS BANK : Level 3   Shape and space   Page 157

MASTERSHEET A50

ACTIVITY

Name: _____ Date: _____ Teacher: _____

Here is part of a telephone directory.

Cutts P, 20 Hazel Lane .... Lexton 34098
Cutts P, 13 Lantern Hill, Streptip .... Lexton 34135
Cutts R, 'Hollies', Common End .... Lexton 40034
Cutts S, 2 Bowness Rd .... Lexton 34569
Cutts & Dixon, Solicitors, Priests Court, West Lane .... Stippley 7892
Cutweld Services Ltd, Unit 1, Leeland Ind. Est. .... Denton 21567
Cyprus Fish Bar, 178 Melton Rd .... Lexton 40654
Czibak W.G, 23 Preston Ave, Coxmore .... Antoth 4231
D&A Driving School, 14 St. Mary's St, Denton .... Denton 21570
D.E.L, T.V Repairs, High St, Denton .... Denton 29849
D.T Concrete, Albert Sq, Frixloxton .... Riplow 364420
D&W Carpets, Main St, Little Gonghits .... Antoth 4888
Dabbs Dr.L, The Surgery, Milltown .... Stippley 7123
Dacey P.W.T, 37 Liptin Hill .... Lexton 34543
Dack E, 45 The Common .... Lexton 40400
Dack & Jones, Painting & Decorating,
  3 Thrupter Grove, Bentip .... Bentip 2157

What is the telephone number of Simon Cutts? _____

Whose telephone number is Antoth 4231? _____

Who are painters and decorators? _____

Who lives in Milltown? _____

What is the doctor's telephone number? _____

Evaluation: Teacher's comment:

can extract information from lists;
can interpret information in a list

See Activity 103 (p.81)

Page 158   Handling data   **MATHS BANK: Level 3**

MATHS BANK 3
LEVEL THREE

Handling data

Nelson

MASTERSHEET A51

Name: _____ Date: _____ Teacher: _____

Here is part of a train timetable.

London to Derby

Monday to Friday		**Saturdays**		**Sundays**	
London St. Pancras	Derby	London St. Pancras	Derby	London St. Pancras	Derby
depart	arrive	depart	arrive	depart	arrive
0700	**0845**	**0700**	**0840**	**0830**	**1110**
0800	**0945**	**0830**	**1015**	**1130**	**1354**
0900	**1047**	**1000**	**1145**	**1330**	**1540**
1000	**1141**	**1130**	**1310**	**1530**	**1732**
1100	**1255**	**1300**	**1440**	**1705**	**1850**
1200	**1350**	**1430**	**1615**	**1805**	**1960**
1300	**1450**	**1600**	**1740**		
1400	**1560**	**1700**	**1840**		
1500	**1645**	**1800**	**1940**		
1600	**1740**				
1700	**1830**				
1730	**1930**				
1800	**1940**				

(Note: this timetable is not real.)

What time does the 1730 train arrive in Derby? _____

Which train arrives in Derby at 1440 on a Saturday? _____

How long should the 0800 train take to reach Derby on a Monday? _____

How many trains arrive at Derby before 12 noon on a weekday? _____

Evaluation:
can extract information from lists and tables;
can interpret information in a list and table

Teacher's comment:

See Activity 104 (p.81)

MATHS BANK: Level 3   Handling data   Page 159

MASTERSHEET A52

ACTIVITY

Name: _____ Date: _____ Teacher: _____

Jones's Ices
- Small cornets 30p
- Large cornets 45p
- Wafers 35p
- Choc ices 60p
- Tubs 50p
- Lolly tube 30p
- Drink on a Stick 25p
- Zoom bar 35p

Marino's Ices
- Small Cornets 32p
- Large Cornets 44p
- Wafers 35p
- Choc ices 60p
- Tubs 45p
- Lolly tube 32p
- Drink on a stick 42p
- Zoom bar 40p

Who sells the cheaper Zoom bar? _____

How much would a small and a large cornet cost from Marino's? _____

How much would two choc ices cost from Jones's? _____

How many wafers for one pound from Marino's? _____

How much more do three small cornets cost from Marino's than from Jones's? _____

Evaluation:
can extract information from lists;
can interpret information in a list

Teacher's comment:

See Activity 105 (p.81)

Handling data

MATHS BANK: Level 3

MASTERSHEET A53

Name: _____ Date: _____ Teacher: _____

Here is a football league table.

	Home						**Away**					
	P	W	D	L	F	A	W	D	L	F	A	Pts
Liverpool	20	9	1	0	26	5	6	2	2	15	11	48
Arsenal	21	8	2	0	25	5	6	5	0	16	5	47
C.Palace	21	7	3	0	16	9	5	3	3	15	11	42
Leeds	21	7	2	2	24	10	4	4	2	12	11	39
Man.U.	21	6	2	3	19	10	4	4	2	13	13	35
Tottenham	21	7	2	2	26	15	2	4	4	8	12	33
Man.City	20	6	1	3	16	13	1	7	2	14	15	29
Chelsea	21	6	4	1	18	13	2	1	7	16	26	29
Wimbledon	21	4	4	3	15	14	3	3	4	16	17	28
Norwich	20	6	1	3	16	15	2	1	7	8	18	26
Everton	21	5	3	3	16	9	1	3	6	8	16	24
Nottm. Forest	19	4	2	3	15	13	2	4	4	12	16	24
Aston Villa	20	4	5	0	13	6	1	3	7	7	14	23
Luton	21	4	4	2	11	7	2	1	8	11	25	23
Southampton	21	5	2	3	18	12	1	2	8	11	25	22
Coventry	21	4	4	3	16	12	1	2	7	5	13	21
Sunderland	21	3	4	4	10	10	1	2	7	14	22	18
Derby	20	2	6	3	13	17	2	0	7	5	18	18
QPR	21	3	2	5	15	15	1	3	7	11	24	17
Sheff.U	20	2	2	5	13	13	1	2	8	6	23	13

P=played W=won D=drawn L=lost F=goals for A=goals against Pts=points

Which team has scored 26 points? _____

Which team has lost 4 games at home? _____

How many draws has Manchester City scored away? _____

How many goals has Liverpool scored at home and away? _____

Evaluation:
can extract information from tables;
can interpret information in a table

Teacher's comment:

See Activity 106 (p.81)

MATHS BANK: Level 3   Handling data   Page 161

MASTERSHEET A54

ACTIVITY

Name: _____ Date: _____ Teacher: _____

Here is a multiplication table.

x	1	2	3	4	5	6	7	8	9	10
1	1	2	3	4	5	6	7	8	9	10
2	2	4	6	8	10	12	14	16	18	20
3	3	6	9	12	15	18	21	24	27	30
4	4	8	12	16	20	24	28	32	36	40
5	5	10	15	20	25	30	35	40	45	50
6	6	12	18	24	30	36	42	48	54	60
7	7	14	21	28	35	42	49	56	63	70
8	8	16	24	32	40	48	56	64	72	80
9	9	18	27	36	45	54	63	72	81	90
10	10	20	30	40	50	60	70	80	90	100

What is 7×9 equal to? _____

Which pairs of numbers multiplied together give an answer of 45? _____

How many times does 24 appear in the table? _____

Evaluation:
can extract information from tables;
can interpret information in a table

Teacher's comment:

See Activity 107 (p.81)

Handling data

MASTERSHEET A55

Name: _____ Date: _____ Teacher: _____

Several people were asked on which day of the week their birthdays were held.
Draw a graph to show the information.

Days	Sun	Mon	Tue	Wed	Thu	Fri	Sat
Number of people	16	7	23	15	20	8	19

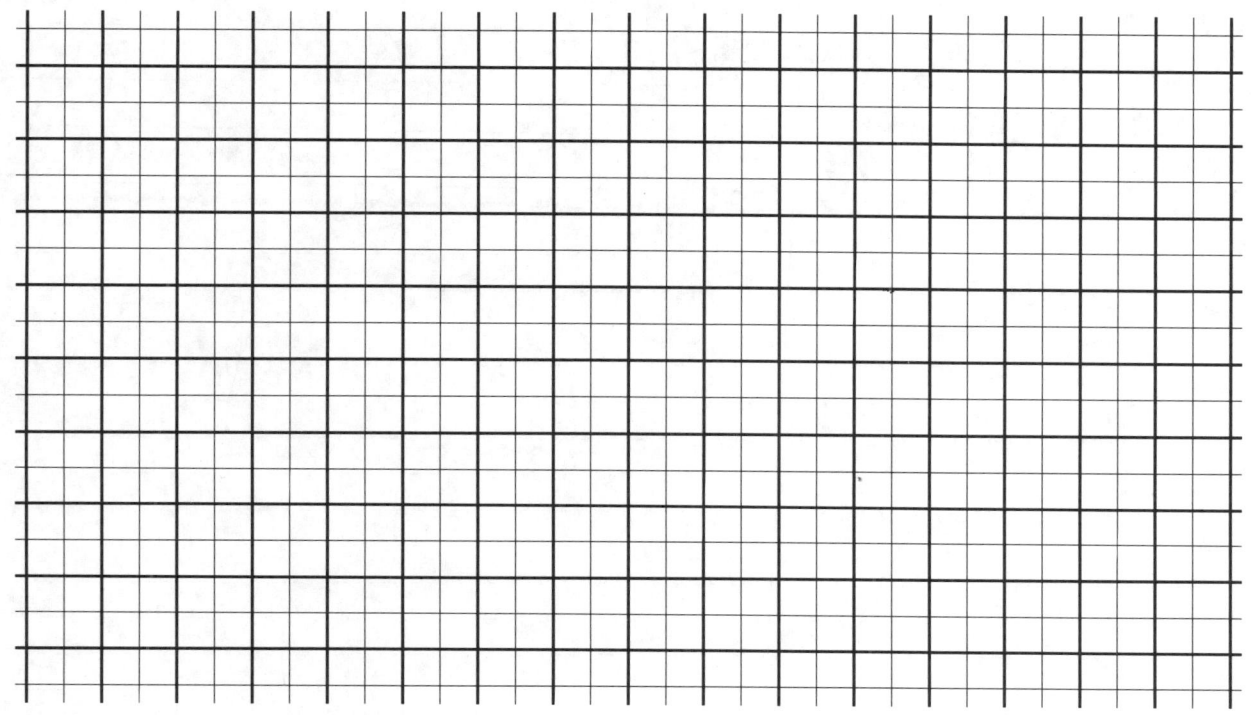

Write two things you can find out from your graph:

_____
_____
_____
_____

Evaluation:
uses sensible scale;
uses appropriate labels;
draws graph correctly;
can interpret graph

Teacher's comment:

See Activity 109 (p.83)

MATHS BANK: Level 3   Handling data

MASTERSHEET A56

Name: _____ Date: _____ Teacher: _____

Here are the results of a traffic survey.
Draw a graph to show the information.

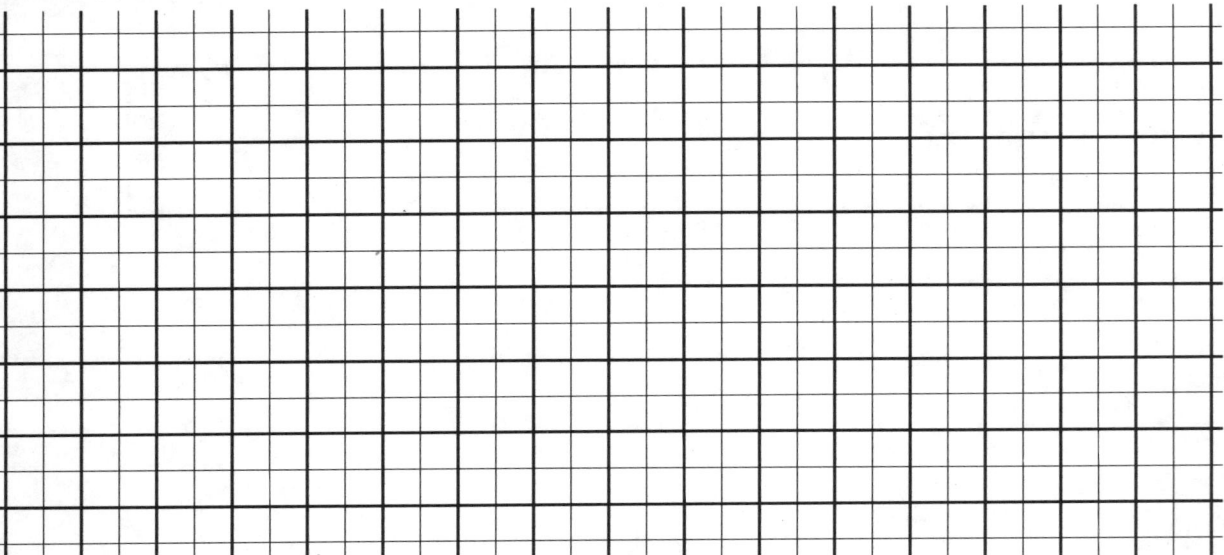

cars																																
vans																	
lorries																						
tankers									
buses			
motor cycles												
pedal cycles			
others							

How many lorries and vans were recorded? _____

What do you think 'other' vehicles could have included? _____

Evaluation: Teacher's comment:
uses sensible scale;
uses appropriate labels;
draws graph correctly;
can interpret graph

See Activity 110 (p.84)

MASTERSHEET A57

ACTIVITY

Name: _____ Date: _____ Teacher: _____

Some people tasted potato crisps and recorded their favourite flavours.
This table shows the results.
Now draw a graph to show the results.

plain	salt 'n vinegar	cheese 'n onion	prawn	tomato	barbecue	smoky bacon
16	12	8	5	9	7	11

Which was the favourite flavour? _____

How many people liked smoky bacon flavour? _____

How many people took part in the tasting? _____

Evaluation:
uses sensible scale

Teacher's comment:

See Activity 111 (p.84)

MATHS BANK: Level 3   Handling data   Page 165

MASTERSHEET A58

Name: _____ Date: _____ Teacher: _____

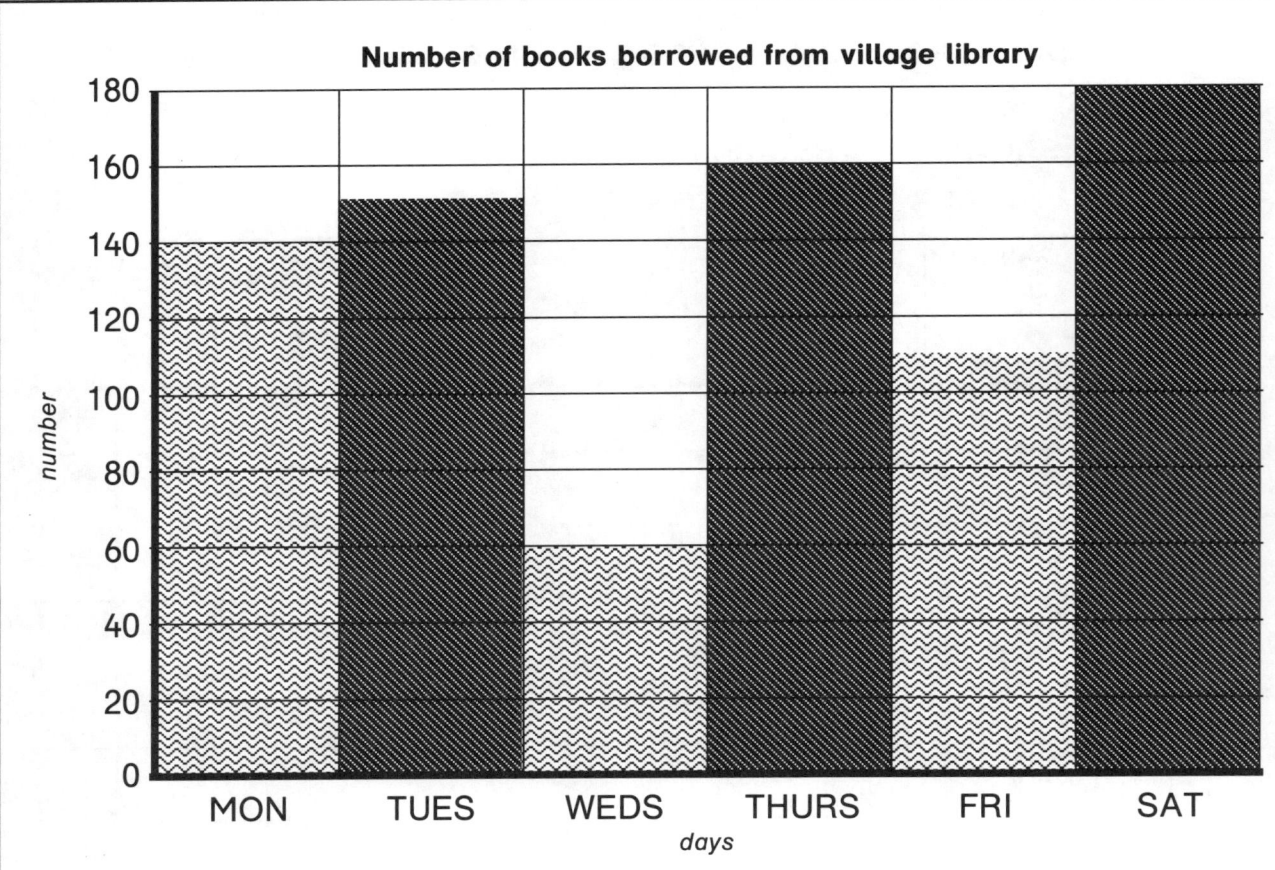

Which was the busiest day? _____

Which day saw 150 books borrowed? _____

Which day do you think was half-day closing for the library? _____

How many books were borrowed during Friday and Saturday? _____

Evaluation:
able to interpret bar chart

Teacher's comment:

See Activity 112 (p.85)

MASTERSHEET A59

Name: _____ Date: _____ Teacher: _____

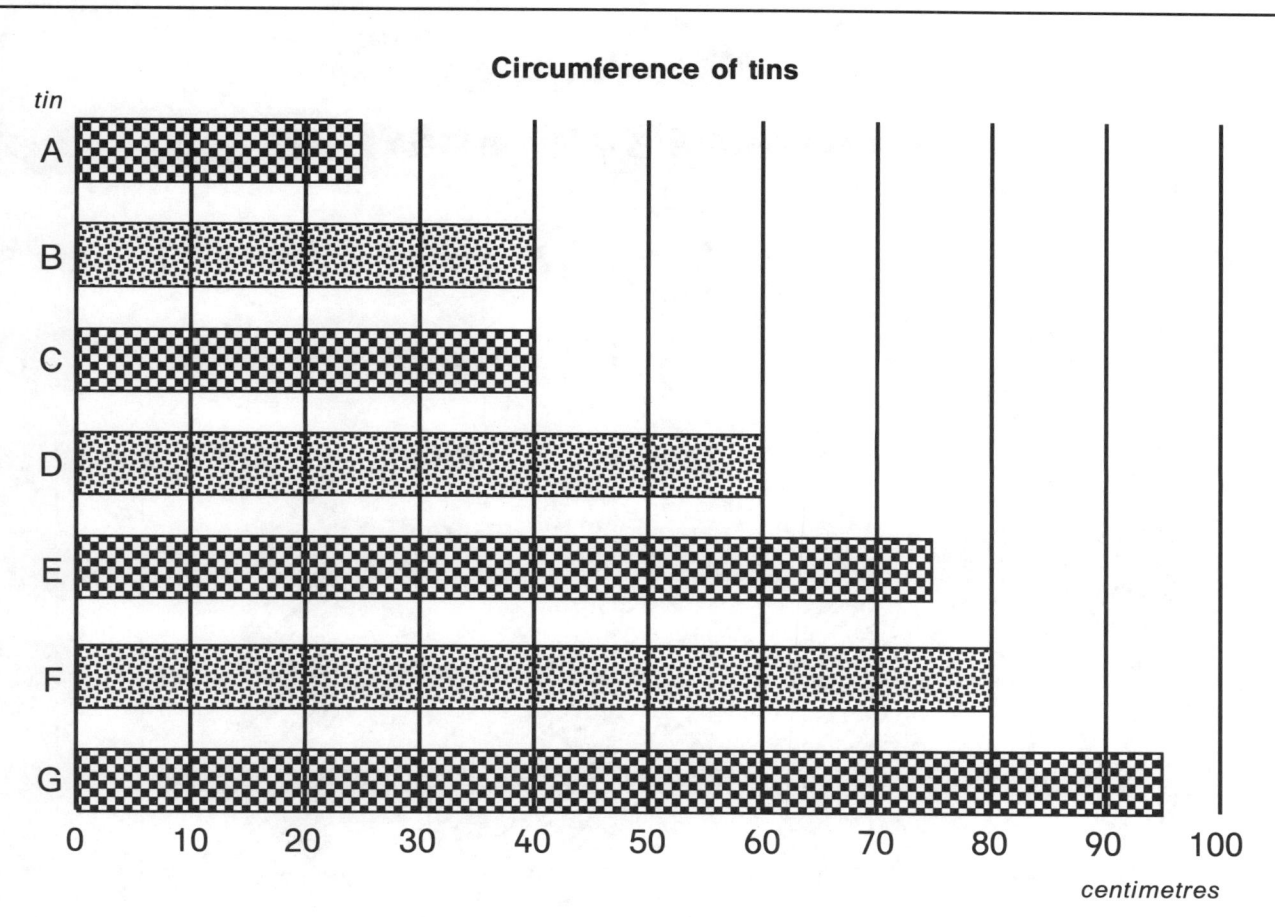

Which tin has a circumference of 75cm? _____

What is the circumference of tin D? _____

Which tins have the same circumferences? _____

Which tins have a shorter circumference than tin E? _____

Evaluation:
able to interpret bar chart

Teacher's comment:

See Activity 113 (p.85)

MASTERSHEET A60

ACTIVITY

Name: _____ Date: _____ Teacher: _____

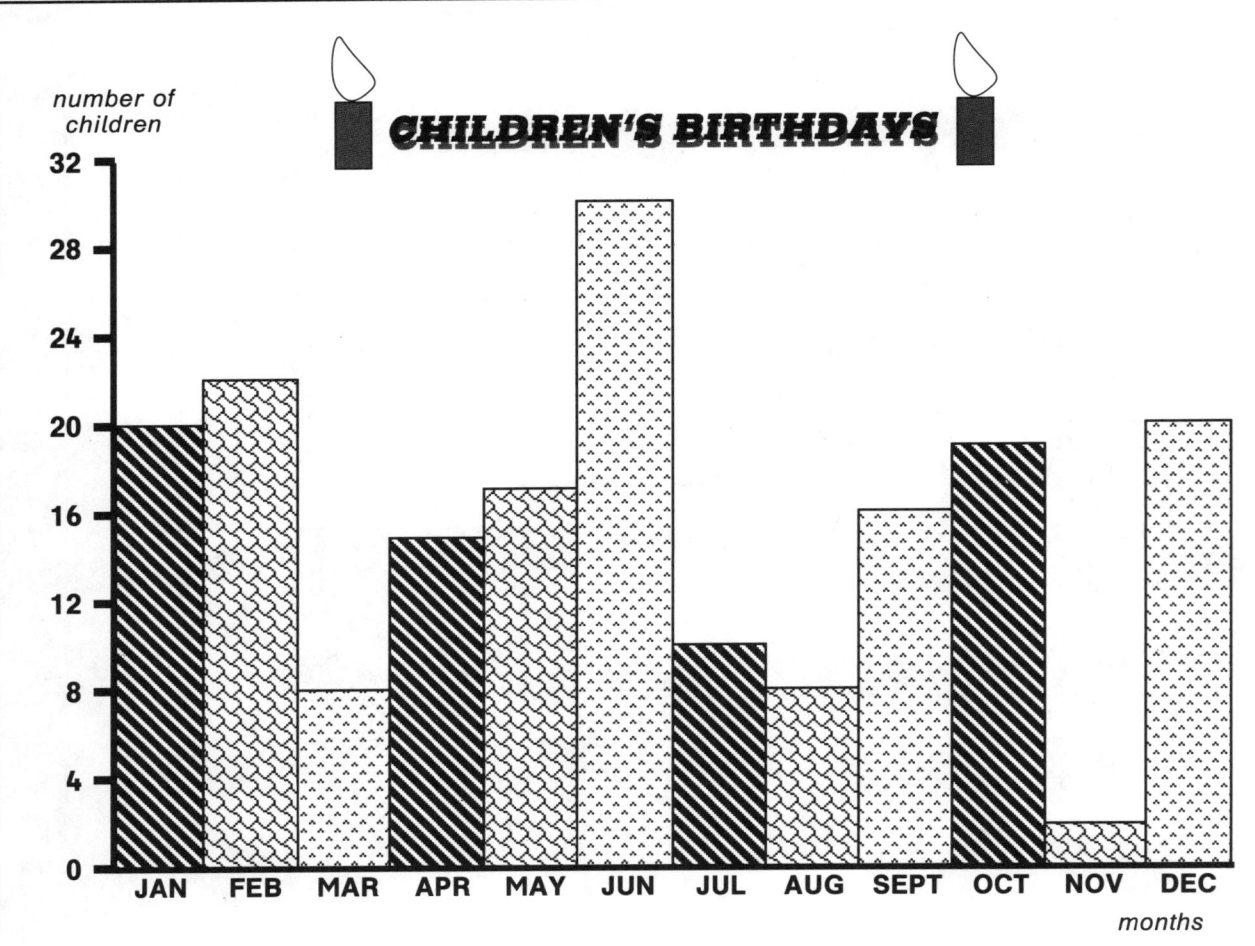

How many children have a birthday in May? _____

Which month has 22 birthdays in it? _____

Which month has fewest birthdays? _____

How many children were asked their birthday month? _____

Evaluation:
able to interpret bar chart

Teacher's comment:

See Activity 114 (p.85)

Handling data

MASTERSHEET A61

ACTIVITY

Name: _____ Date: _____ Teacher: _____

Answer the questions below using information from these pictograms.

Large producers of hi-fi units

[pictogram] is approximately 5 million

Hong Kong, China, Singapore, Japan, USA

Large producers of TV sets

[pictogram] is approximately 2 million

Japan, USA, USSR, S. Korea, China

Which countries make more hi-fi units than Singapore? _____

Which country makes approximately 15 million hi-fi units? _____

Which countries make more than 10 million TV sets? _____

Approximately how many TV sets does South Korea make? _____

Evaluation:
can estimate appropriately;
can interpret a pictogram;
can read scales

Teacher's comment:

See Activity 115 (p.86)

MATHS BANK: Level 3   Handling data   Page 169

MASTERSHEET A62

Name: _____ Date: _____ Teacher: _____

Draw a pictogram to show this information.

Number of people visiting the Multiscreen cinema in one week

Monday	406	Friday	956
Tuesday	679	Saturday	1156
Wednesday	693	Sunday	835
Thursday	521		

Write two things you can find out from the pictogram.

1 _____

2 _____

Evaluation:
can draw appropriate pictogram;
can use part symbols sensibly;
can estimate appropriately;
can interpret a pictogram

Teacher's comment:

See Activity 116 (p.86)

Page 170 Handling data MATHS BANK: Level 3

MASTERSHEET A63

Name: _____ Date: _____ Teacher: _____

Draw a pictogram to show this information.

Bags of crisps eaten by each class during one week

Class 1	102	Class 4	115
Class 2	63	Class 5	89
Class 3	153	Class 6	94

Write two things you can find out from the pictogram.

1 _____

2 _____

Evaluation:
can draw appropriate pictogram;
can use part symbols sensibly;
can estimate appropriately;
can interpret a pictogram

Teacher's comment:

See Activity 117 (p.87)

MATHS BANK : Level 3 Handling data Page 171

MASTERSHEET A64

ACTIVITY

Name: _____ Date: _____ Teacher: _____

Join the pictures to the chance boxes.

| very likely | likely | unlikely | very unlikely |

I shall watch TV tonight

I shall have chips today

I shall brush my teeth today

I shall become a teacher

I shall run in the Olympic Games

Evaluation:
can place events in order of likelihood;
can use appropriate 'chance' words

Teacher's comment:

See Activity 118 (p.88)

Handling data

MATHS BANK: Level 3

MASTERSHEET A65

ACTIVITY

Name: _____ Date: _____ Teacher: _____

What events could go in each box?

certain
_____
_____
_____
_____

possible
_____
_____
_____
_____

doubtful
_____
_____
_____
_____

impossible
_____
_____
_____
_____

Evaluation:
can place events in order of likelihood;
can use appropriate 'chance' words

Teacher's comment:

See Activity 119 (p.88)

MATHS BANK: Level 3 Handling data

MASTERSHEET A66

ACTIVITY

Name: _____ Date: _____ Teacher: _____

Write some words to describe the chance of these things happening to you.

becoming a pop star

chance
_____
_____
_____

going to school tomorrow

chance
_____
_____
_____

flying to the moon

chance
_____
_____
_____

learning to drive

chance
_____
_____
_____

playing a game today

chance
_____
_____
_____

having something to drink today

chance
_____
_____
_____

Evaluation:
decides 'likelihood' sensibly;
uses appropriate words to identify 'chance'

Teacher's comment:

_____

_____

Page 174   Handling data   Maths Bank: Level 3

MASTERSHEET A67

ACTIVITY

Name: _____ Date: _____ Teacher: _____

What apparatus did you use?

What were you trying to get?

What was the chance of getting it?

even ☐   more than even ☐   less than even ☐

Results of experiment

Evaluation:
understands 'evens';
says whether events are more or less likely
than 'evens'

Teacher's comment:

See Activity 121 (p.89)

MATHS BANK : Level 3   Handling data   Page 175

MASTERSHEET A68

ACTIVITY

Name: _____ Date: _____ Teacher: _____

Look at the numbers on the trucks.
Look at the numbers on the wheels.
Can you see the pattern?

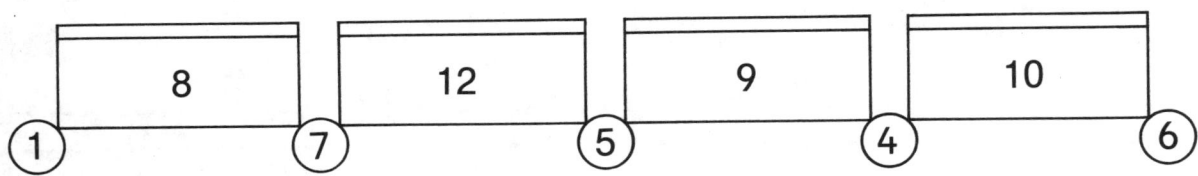

Write as many answers as you can for the wheels of each of these trucks?

A

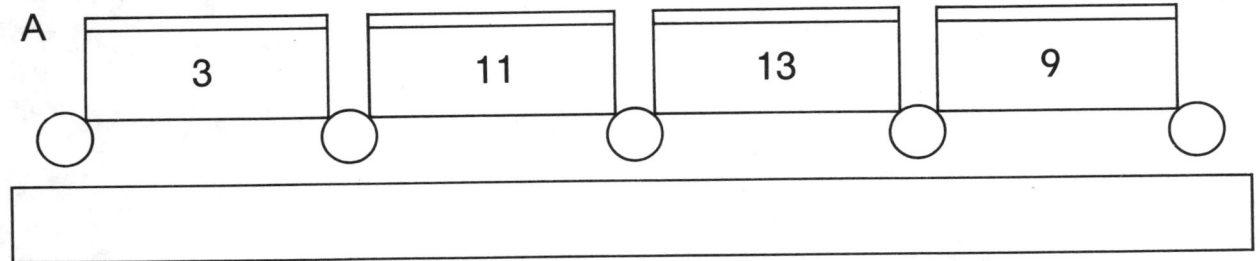

B

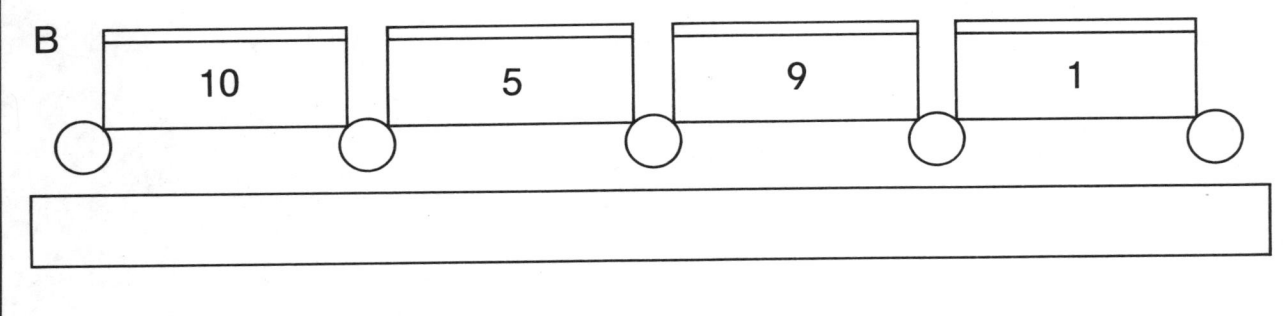

Evaluation: Teacher's comment:

See Activity 128 (p.95)

Page 176 — Using and applying mathematics — **Maths Bank : Level 3**

Maths Bank

LEVEL THREE

Using & applying mathematics

Nelson

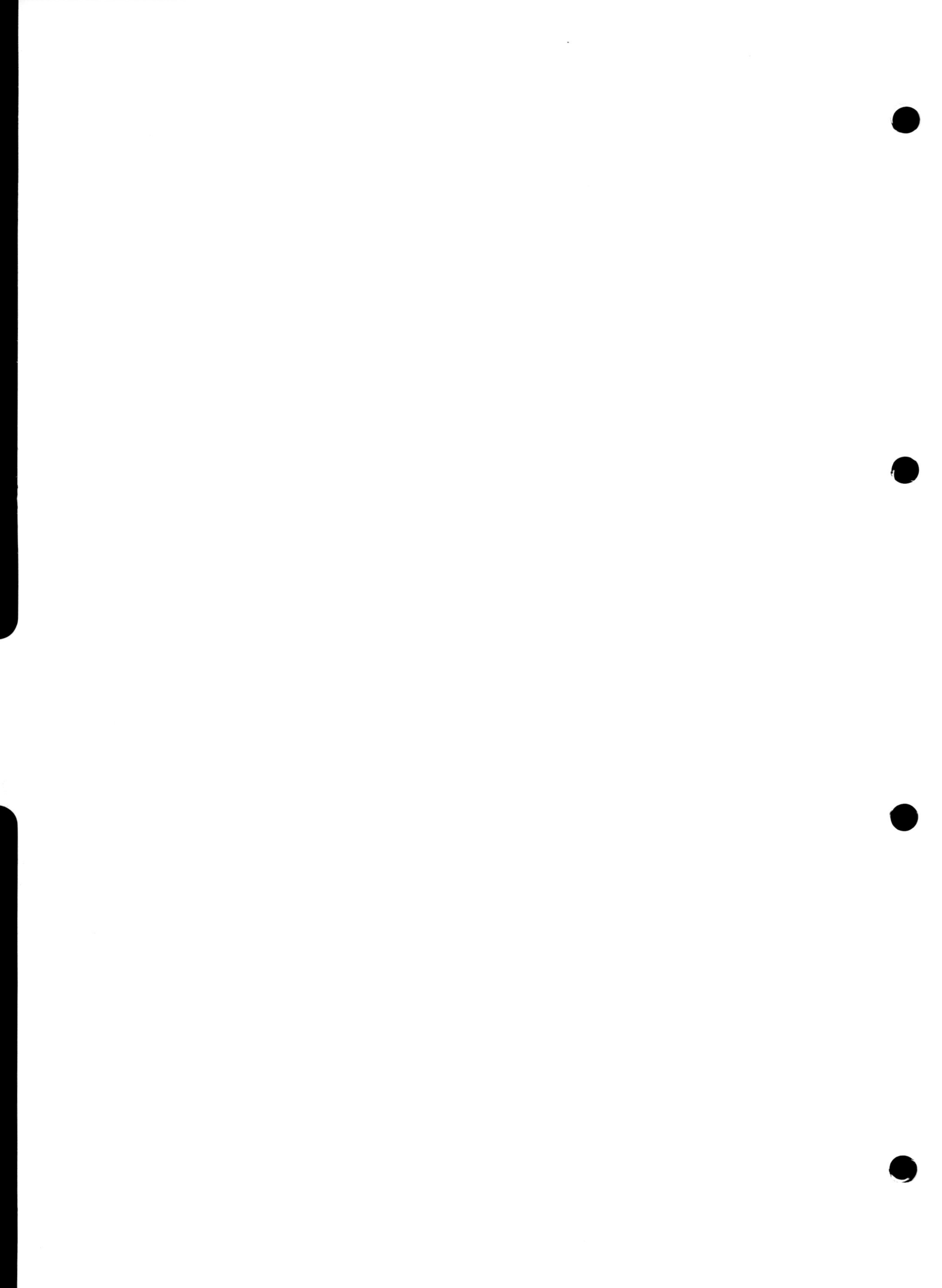

MASTERSHEET A69

ACTIVITY

Name: _____ Date: _____ Teacher: _____

Write some numbers you see around you every day.
Say where you found each number.
Try to explain what the numbers mean.

Evaluation: _____ Teacher's comment: _____

See Activity 130 (p.97)

MATHS BANK: Level 3   Using and applying mathematics   Page 177

MASTERSHEET A70

ACTIVITY

Name: _____ Date: _____ Teacher: _____

Choose a set of 4 number cards and find row totals.

Evaluation: Teacher's comment:

See Activity 132 (p.99)

Page 178   Using and applying mathematics   **MATHS BANK: Level 3**

MASTERSHEET A71

ACTIVITY

Name: _____ Date: _____ Teacher: _____

The totals are shown.
Find number cards to fit on the grids.

A
6
8
9   5

B
5
6
8   3

C
8
6
9   7

D

Evaluation: *Teacher's comment:*

See Activity 133 (p.100)

MATHS BANK: Level 3   Using and applying mathematics   Page 179

MASTERSHEET A72

Name: _____ Date: _____ Teacher: _____

ACTIVITY

How many cubes do you think you need to make each model?

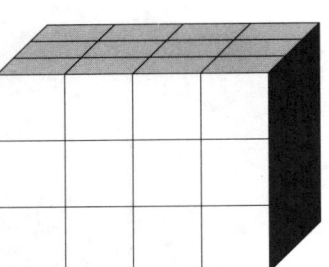
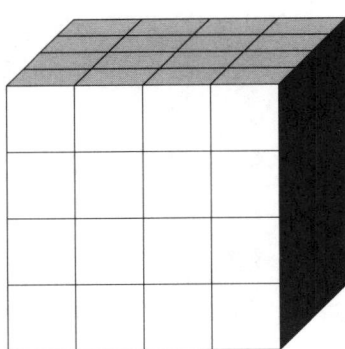
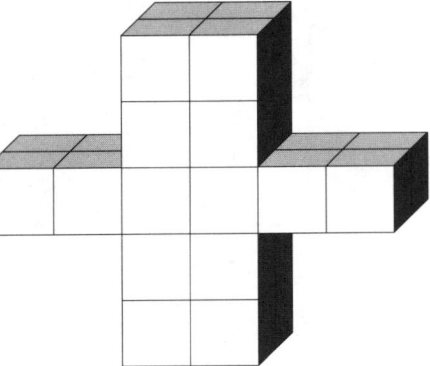
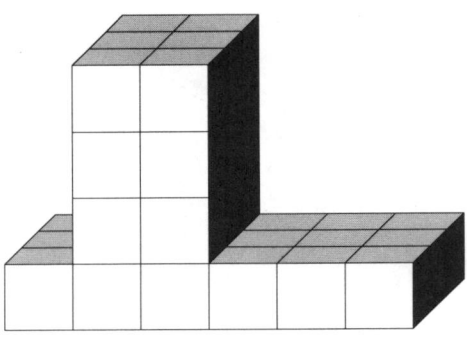
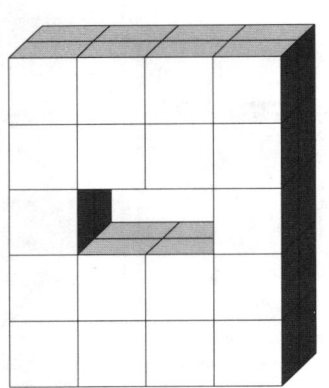
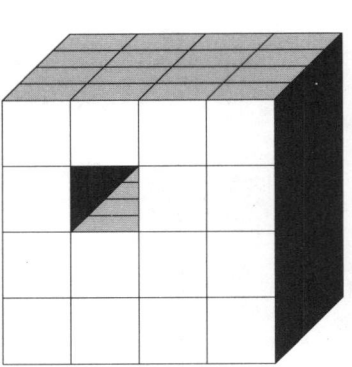

Make each model to check if you were right.

Evaluation: Teacher's comment:

See Activity 134 (p.101)

MASTERSHEET A73

Name: _____ Date: _____ Teacher: _____

Plan a route from a starting point in your classroom to somewhere else in the school or school grounds.
Write the instructions for your *mystery trail*.

follow my mystery trail

Can a friend understand the instructions and follow your mystery trail?

Evaluation: Teacher's comment:

See Activity 136 (p.101)

MASTERSHEET A74

Name: _____ Date: _____ Teacher: _____

Use logic blocks.

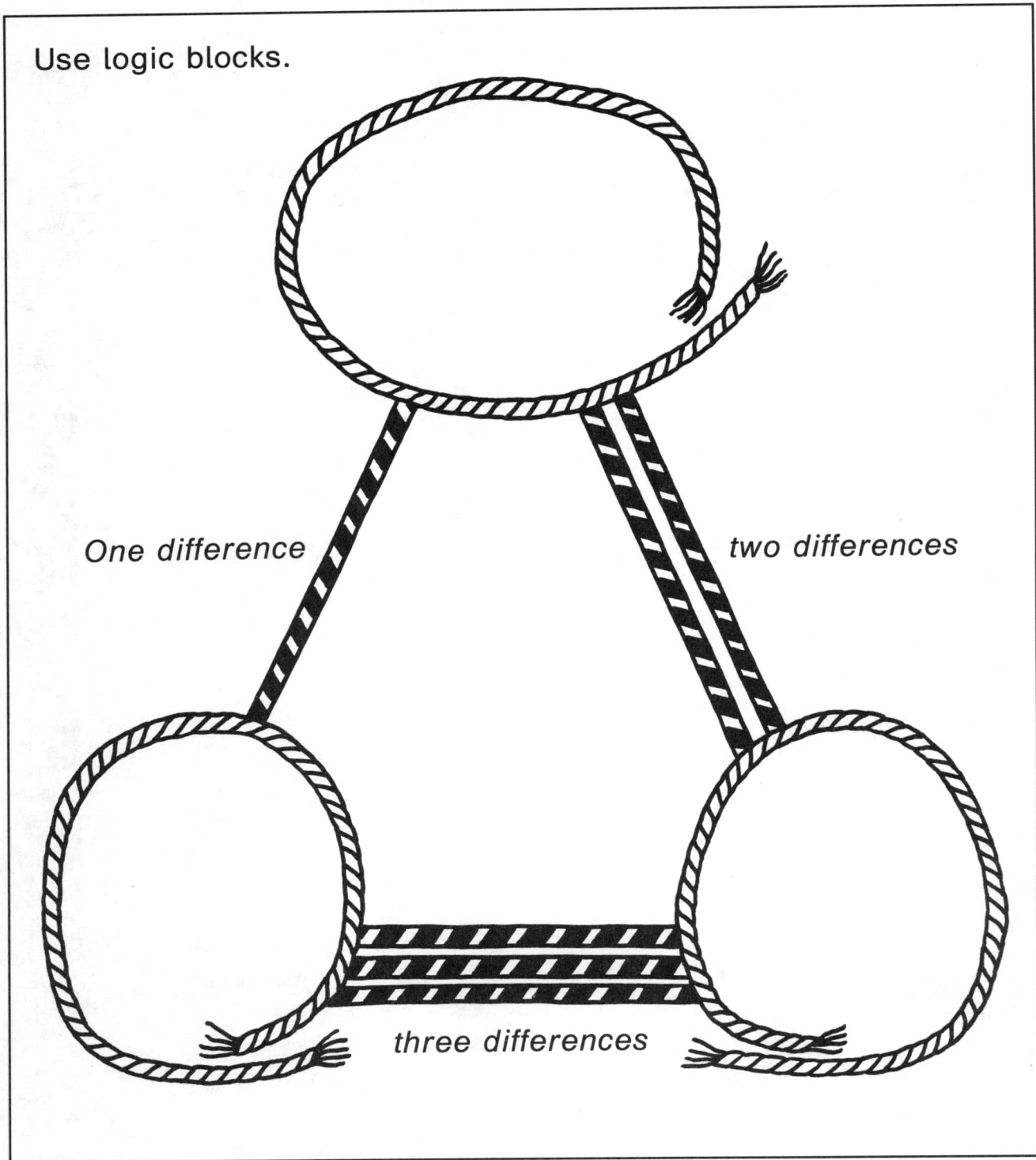

One difference *two differences*

three differences

Evaluation: _____ Teacher's comment: _____

See Activity 140 (p.105)

MASTERSHEET A75

ACTIVITY

Name: _____ Date: _____ Teacher: _____

Use logic blocks.

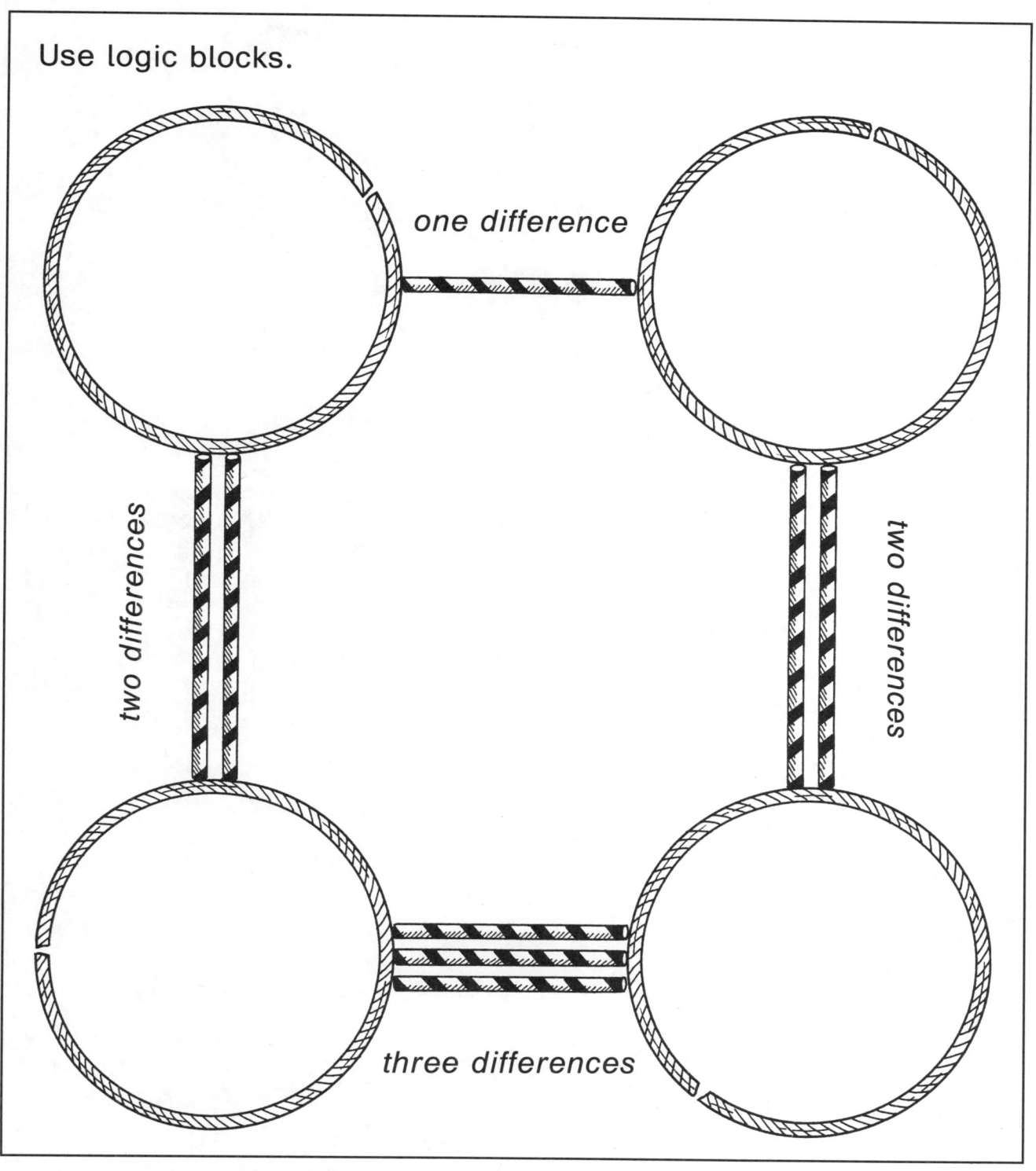

Evaluation: Teacher's comment:

See Activity 141 (p.105)

MATHS BANK: Level 3   Using and applying mathematics   Page 183

MATHS BANK

LEVEL THREE

Resource Mastersheets B1 – 8
These sheets provide support materials in certain activities if suitable material is not available in the classroom.

Appendix B

Nelson

MASTERSHEET B1

ACTIVITY

Fan numbers

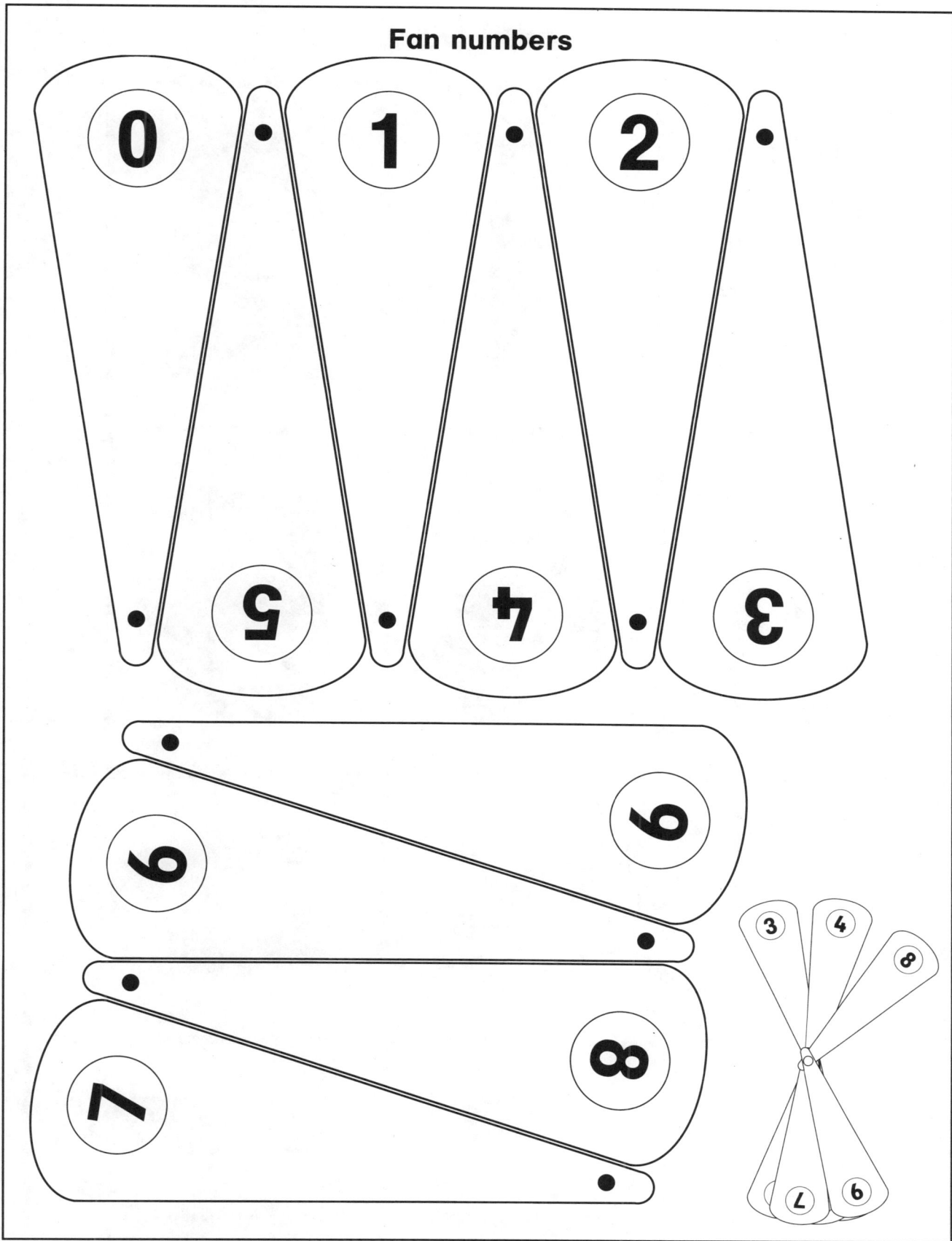

See Activities 1 and 2 (pp.9 – 10)

MATHS BANK: Level 3

MASTERSHEET B2

ACTIVITY

Digit cards

0	1	2
3	4	5
7	9
6	8

See Activities 3, 4, 5 (pp.11 – 12), 34 (p.29), 49 (p.41)

MATHS BANK : Level 3

MASTERSHEET B3

Base 10 apparatus

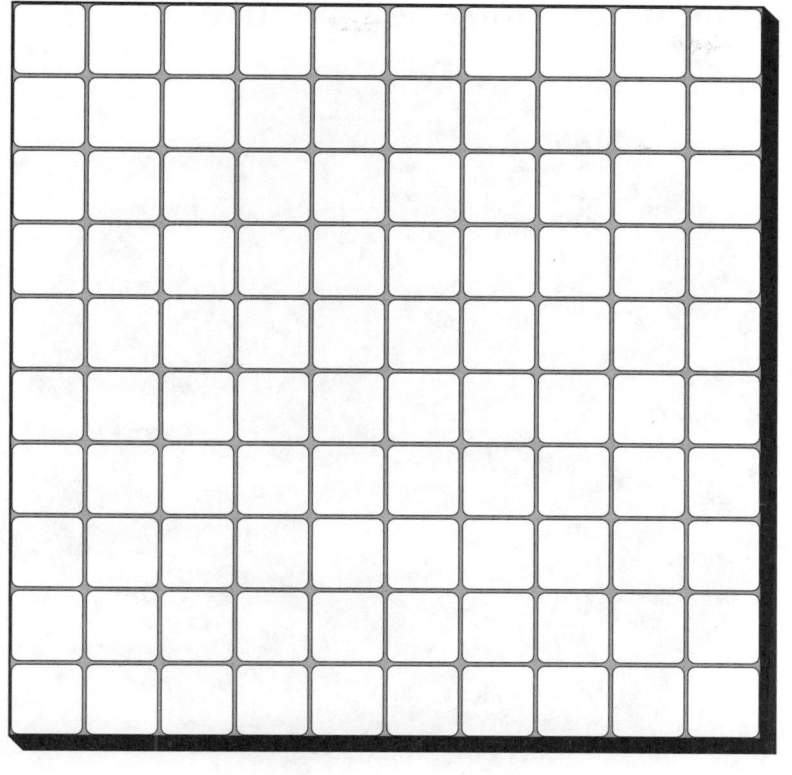

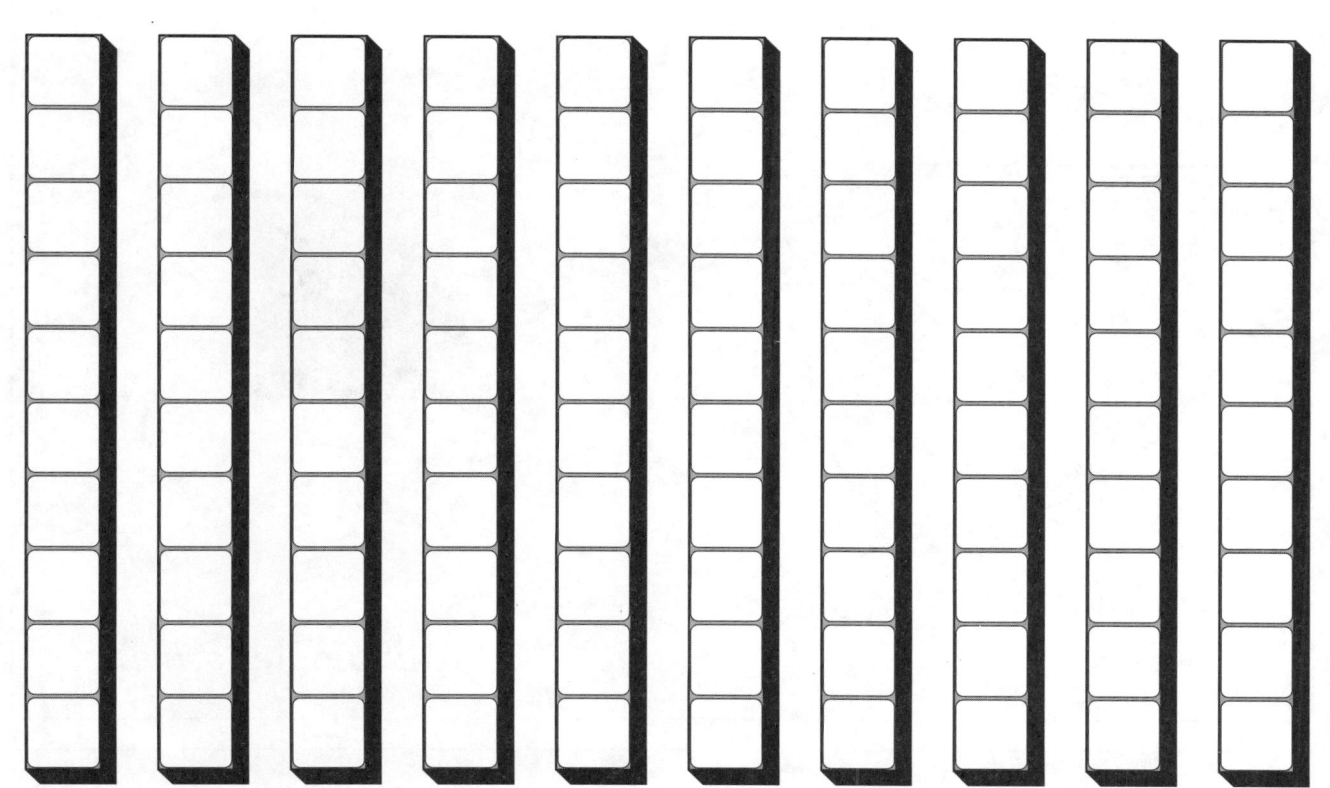

See Activity 11 (p.16)

MASTERSHEET B4

Cut these two circles out.
Cut along each line and fit the circles together to make an angle-former.

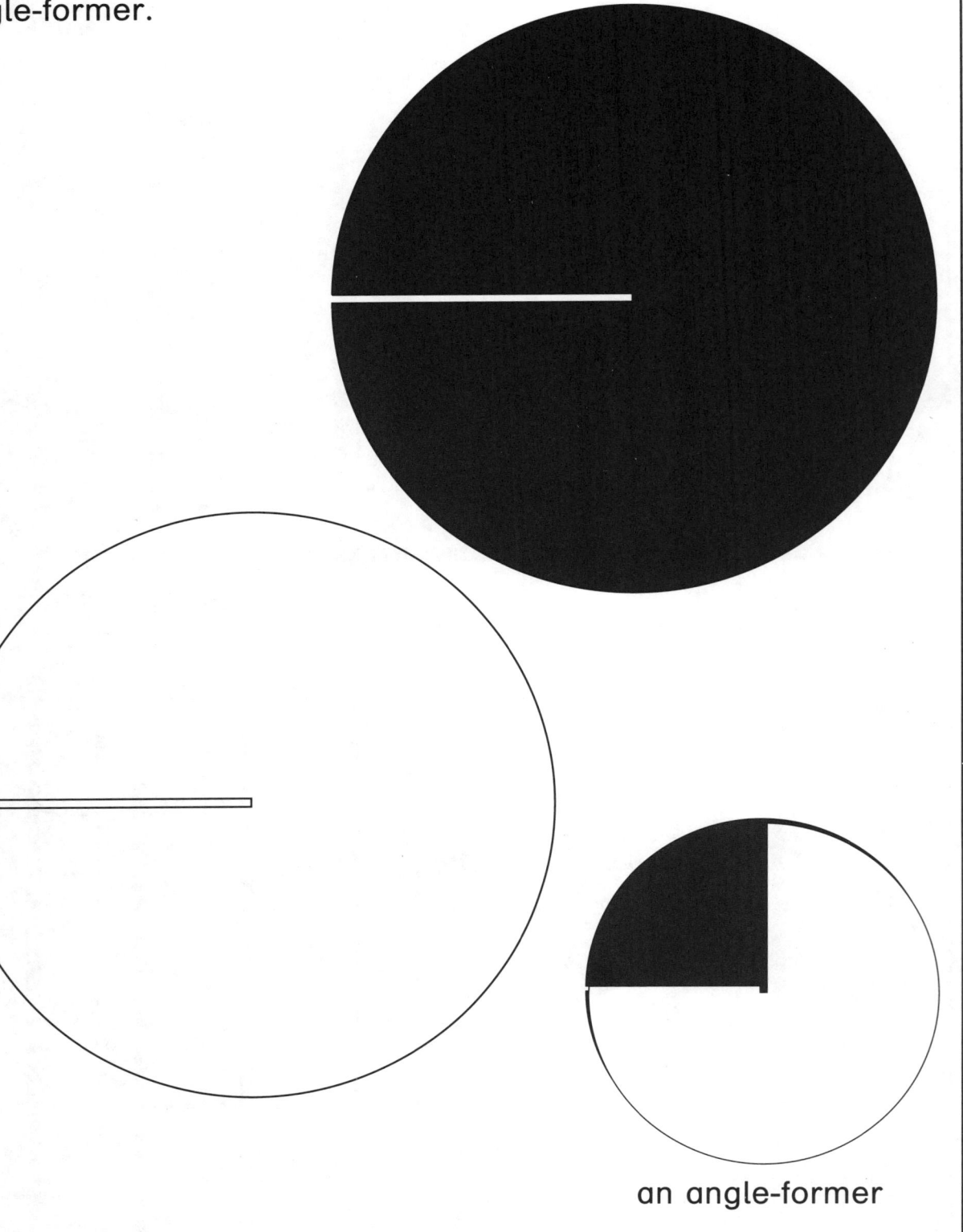

an angle-former

See Activity 101 (p.77)

MASTERSHEET B5

ACTIVITY

Cut out the circle and pointer.
Clip them together with a fastener in the middle.

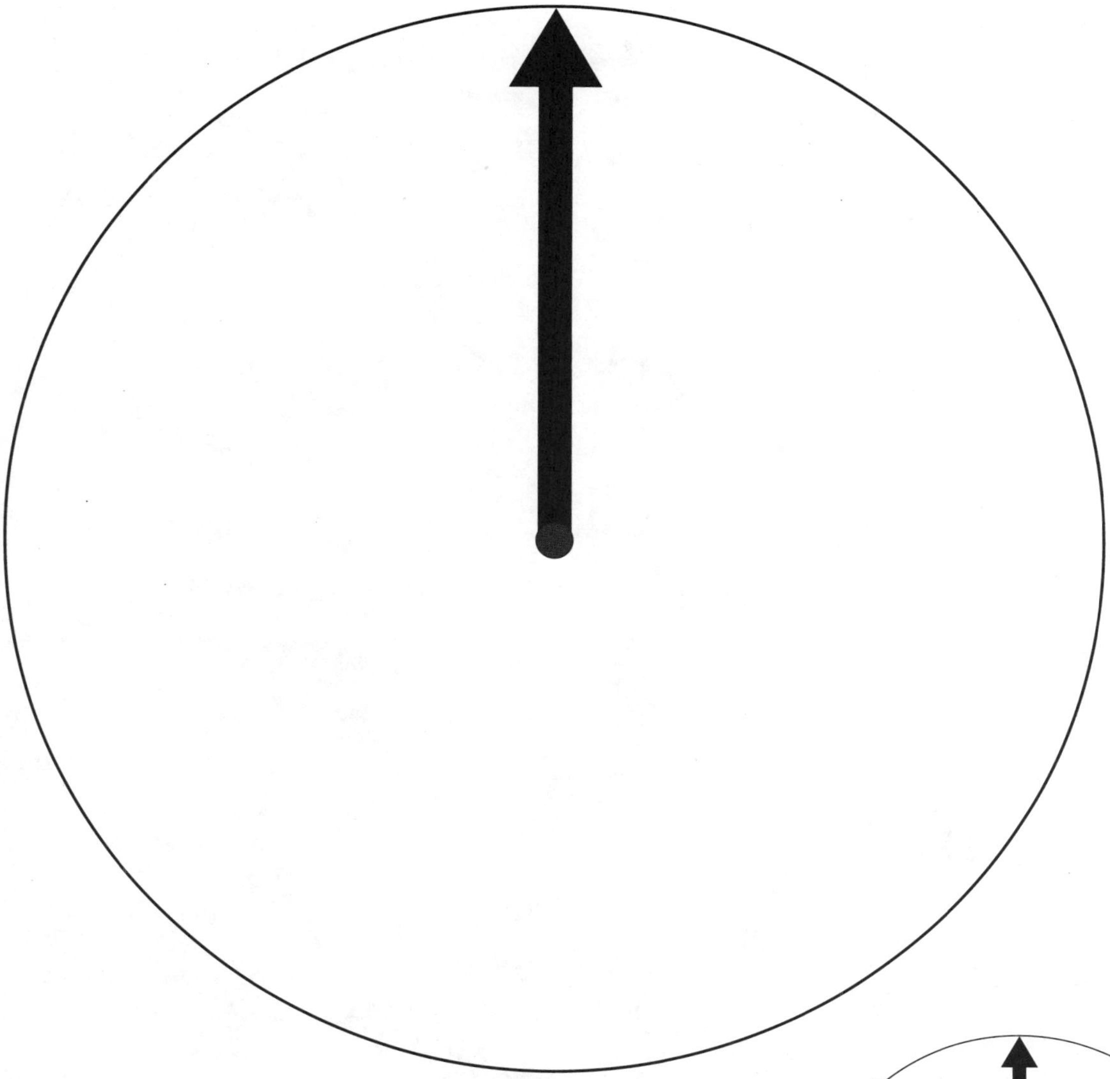

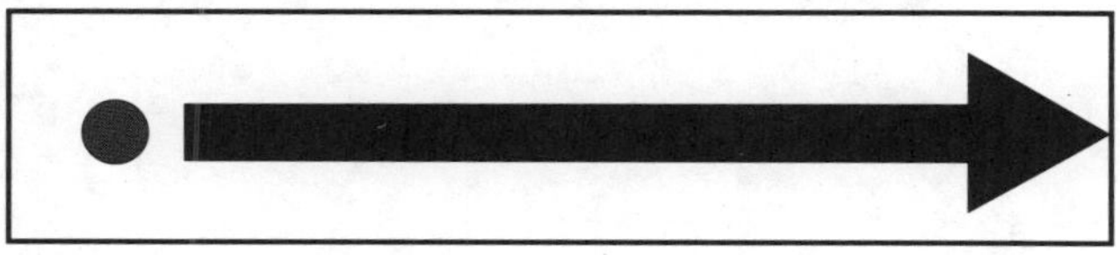

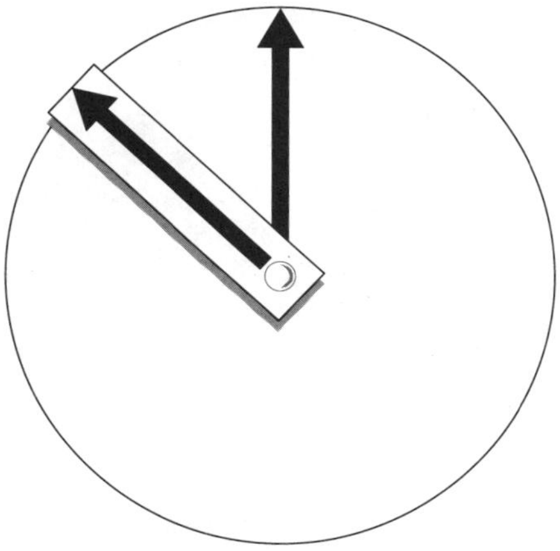

See Activity 102 (p.78)

MATHS BANK: Level 3

MASTERSHEET B6

ACTIVITY

Spinners

Note: Ensure that the spinners are made accurately, otherwise the games will be biased.

See Activities 121 (p.89), 125 (p.91)

MASTERSHEET B7

Numeral cards

0	1	2	3	4	5	6
7	8	9	10	11	12	13
14	15	16	17	18	19	20

0	1	2	3	4	5	6
7	8	9	10	11	12	13
14	15	16	17	18	19	20

See Activities 132, 133 (pp.99 – 100)

MASTERSHEET B8

ACTIVITY

Cut out the large triangle.
Fold along the lines.

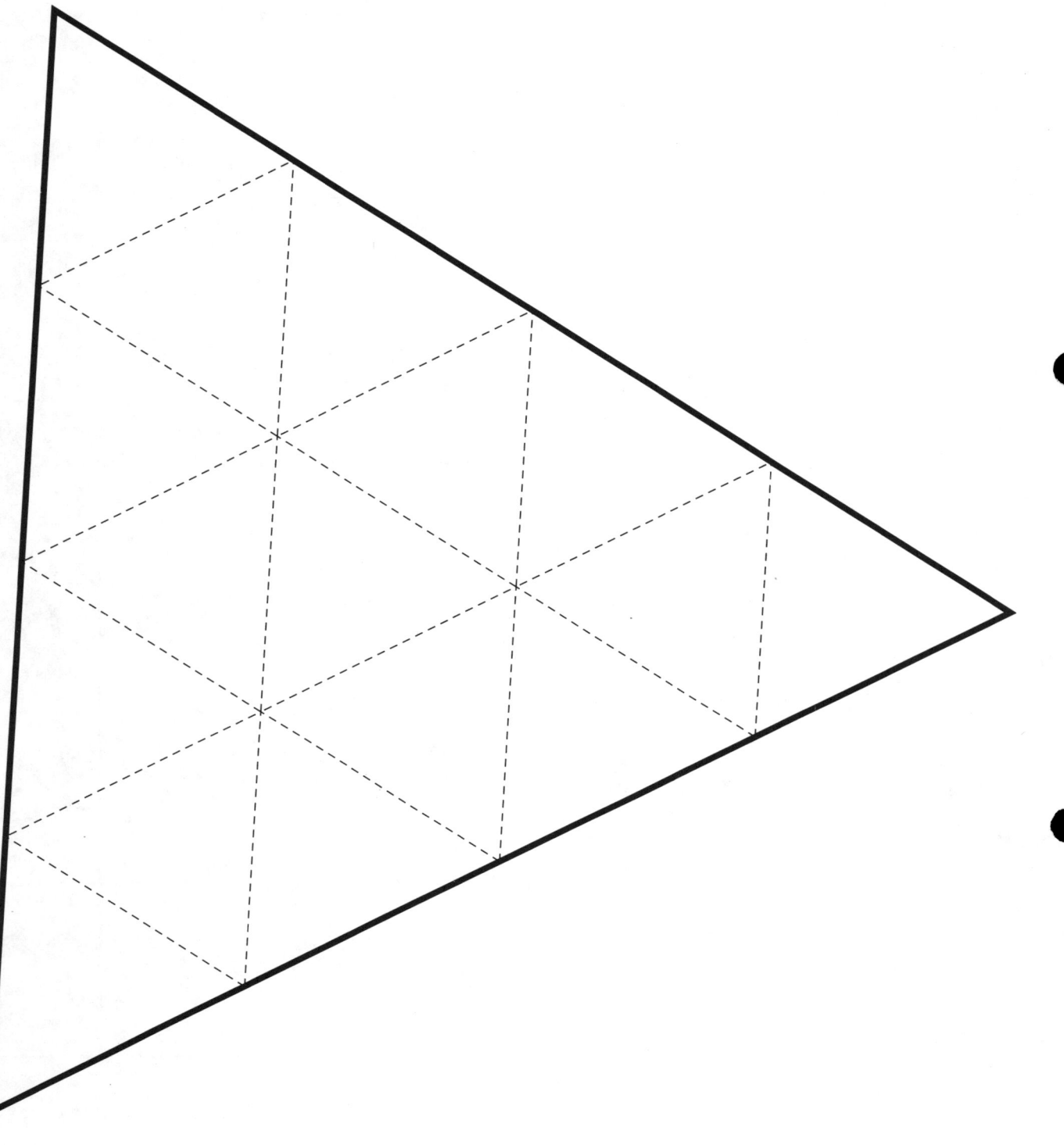

See Activity 142 (p.106)

Page 192

MATHS BANK: Level 3

Recording Mastersheets C1 – 8
These sheets are for pupils and/or teachers to record what has been achieved in any given activity.

Record charts 1–6

Overview

Nelson

MASTERSHEET C1

ACTIVITY

Name: _____ Date: _____ Teacher: _____

Recording sheet

Evaluation: 					Teacher's comment:

Pupils may record their results on this sheet, when appropriate.

MATHS BANK : Level 3 					Page 193

© A. Brighouse, D. Godber, P. Patilla 1992. Copying permitted for purchasing schools only. Published by Thomas Nelson and Sons Ltd.

MASTERSHEET C2

ACTIVITY

Name: _____ Date: _____ Teacher: _____

Recording sheet

Evaluation: Teacher's comment:

Pupils may record their results on this sheet, when appropriate.

Page 194   Maths Bank: Level 3

MASTERSHEET C3

ACTIVITY

Name: _____ Date: _____ Teacher: _____

Recording sheet

Evaluation: Teacher's comment:

Pupils may record their results on this sheet, when appropriate.

MASTERSHEET C4

Name: _____ Date: _____ Teacher: _____

Observation and evaluation sheet

Task

Observations

Attainment targets and levels evaluated

Page 196

MATHS BANK: Level 3

MASTERSHEET C5

ACTIVITY

Name: _____ Date: _____ Teacher: _____

Table of measurements

What was measured	Unit used	Estimate	Measurement

Evaluation: Teacher's comment:

See Activities 55, 56 (p.47), 58, 59 (p.49) 61, 63 (pp.51, 52) 64, 65, 66 (pp.53 – 4)

Maths Bank: Level 3   Measures   Page 197

© A. Brighouse, D. Godber, P. Patilla 1992. Copying permitted for purchasing schools only. Published by Thomas Nelson and Sons Ltd.

MASTERSHEET C6

Name: _____ Date: _____ Teacher: _____

Evaluation of using a Database

Name of Database Program

Title of topic

Entering data

Accessing data

General comments

See Activity 108 (p.82)

MASTERSHEET C7

Name: _____ Date: _____ Teacher: _____

What we have to use:

What we have to do:

Do we think it is a 'fair' game?

What happens when the game is played?

Evaluation: *Teacher's comment:*

See Activity 127 (p.92)

MATHS BANK: Level 3

MASTERSHEET C8

ACTIVITY

Name: _____ Date: _____ Teacher: _____

Evaluation: Teacher's comment:

See Activities 142 (p.106), 143 (p.107)

Page 200

MATHS BANK : Level 3

Record chart, part 1

photocopy

NUMBER and ALGEBRA

ATTAINMENT TARGET 2

Name	Activity ▲	1	2	3	4	5	6	7	8	9	10	11	12	13	14	15	16	17	18	19	20	21	22	23	24	25

The overview on pages 207 – 8 relates the activities to the various statements of attainment.

© A. Brighouse, D. Godber, P. Patilla 1992. Copying permitted for purchasing schools only. Published by Thomas Nelson and Sons Ltd.

MATHS BANK: Level 3

Record chart, part 2

NUMBER and ALGEBRA

Name / Activity	ATTAINMENT TARGET 2 — 26 27 28 29 30 31 32 33 34 35 36 37 38 39 40 41	ATTAINMENT TARGET 3 — 42 43 44 45 46 47 48 49 50 51 52 53 54

The overview on pages 207 – 8 relates the activities to the various statements of attainment.

© A. Brighouse, D. Godber, P. Patilla 1992. Copying permitted for purchasing schools only. Published by Thomas Nelson and Sons Ltd.

Page 202 — Maths Bank: Level 3

Record chart, part 3

photocopy

MEASURES

ATTAINMENT TARGET 2

Name	Activity ▲	55	56	57	58	59	60	61	62	63	64	65	66	67	68	69	70	71	72	73	74	75	76

The overview on pages 207 – 8 relates the activities to the various statements of attainment.

© A. Brighouse, D. Godber, P. Patilla 1992. Copying permitted for purchasing schools only. Published by Thomas Nelson and Sons Ltd.

MATHS BANK: Level 3

Record chart, part 4

SHAPE and SPACE — ATTAINMENT TARGET 4

Name / Activity ▲	77	78	79	80	81	82	83	84	85	86	87	88	89	90	91	92	93	94	95	96	97	98	99	100	101	102

© A. Brighouse, D. Godber, P. Patilla 1992. Copying permitted for purchasing schools only. Published by Thomas Nelson and Sons Ltd.

The overview on pages 207 – 8 relates the activities to the various statements of attainment.

Maths Bank: Level 3

Record chart, part 5

photocopy

HANDLING DATA

ATTAINMENT TARGET 5

Activity / Name	103	104	105	106	107	108	109	110	111	112	113	114	115	116	117	118	119	120	121	122	123	124	125	126	127

The overview on pages 207 – 8 relates the activities to the various statements of attainment.

© A. Brighouse, D. Godber, P. Patilla 1992. Copying permitted for purchasing schools only. Published by Thomas Nelson and Sons Ltd.

Maths Bank: Level 3

Page 205

Record chart, part 6

photocopy

USING and APPLYING MATHEMATICS

ATTAINMENT TARGET 1

Name / Activity	128	129	130	131	132	133	134	135	136	137	138	139	140	141	142	143	144	145	146	147

© A. Brighouse, D. Godber, P. Patilla 1992. Copying permitted for purchasing schools only. Published by Thomas Nelson and Sons Ltd.

The overview on pages 207 – 8 relates the activities to the various statements of attainment.

Page 206

MATHS BANK : Level 3

Overview

This overview relates the activities in *Maths Bank* to the various statements of attainment for National Curriculum, Level 3.

		Activities
Attainment Target 2: Number		
Statement (a)	Read, write and order numbers to at least 1000[1]	1 – 12, 19 – 27
Statement (b)	Demonstrate that they know and can use multiplication tables	31 – 33
Statement (c)	Solve problems involving multiplication or division	28 – 30, 39 – 41
Statement (d)	Make estimates based on familiar units of measurement, checking results	34 – 38, 55 – 66, 70 – 76
Statement (e)	Interpret a range of numbers in the context of measurement or money	13 – 18, 55 – 69
Attainment Target 3: Algebra		
Statement (a)	Use pattern in number when doing mental calculations	42 – 51
Statement (b)	Use inverse operations in a simple context	52 – 54
Attainment Target 4: Shape and space		
Statement (a)	Sort shapes using mathematical criteria and give reasons	77 – 89
Statement (b)	Recognise reflective symmetry	
Statement (c)	Use the eight points of the compass to show direction	90 – 102
Attainment Target 5: Handling data		
Statement (a)	Access information in a simple database	103 – 108
Statement (b)	Construct and interpret statistical diagrams	109 – 117
Statement (c)	Use appropriate language to justify decisions when placing events in order of 'likelihood'	118 – 127

---

[1] All statements of attainment have been taken from the document entitled *'Mathematics in the National Curriculum (1991)'* published by HMSO.

Attainment Target 1: Using and applying mathematics

Statement (a)　　Find ways of overcoming difficulties when solving problems

Statement (b)　　Use or interpret appropriate mathematical terms and mathematical aspects of everyday language in a precise way　　128 – 147

Statement (c)　　Present results in a clear and organised way

Statement (d)　　Investigate general statements by trying out some examples